The Anita Bryant Story

BY ANITA BRYANT

Mine Eyes Have Seen the Glory
Amazing Grace
Bless This House
The Anita Bryant Story

BY ANITA BRYANT AND BOB GREEN

Fishers of Men
Light My Candle
Running the Good Race
Raising God's Children

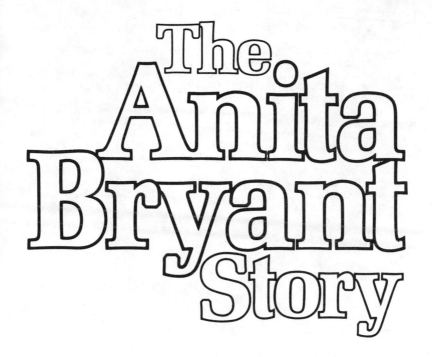

The Anita Bryant Story

The Survival of Our Nation's Families
and the Threat of Militant Homosexuality

by **Anita Bryant**

Fleming H. Revell Company
Old Tappan, New Jersey

You may write to Anita Bryant: Anita Bryant, Miami Beach, Florida 33140.

ISBN 0-8007-0897-0

Copyright © 1977 by Anita Bryant
Published by Fleming H. Revell Company
Library of Congress Card Catalog Number: 77-88806
All rights reserved
Printed in the United States of America

Contents

Foreword

(A word of explanation about this rather unusual foreword—a letter from a young woman we have never met. Later we found out that she is blind. Her letter says so well what we have been through and what we hope this book will accomplish.)

Dear Anita and Bob:

In the recent past I had the opportunity to receive a spiritual blessing—and an education as well—in coming to know two wonderful people, servants of God.

I transcribed the majority of tapes on your forthcoming book, and I have done no work that brought me greater pleasure. Anita, your singing is not only beautiful, but moving, and I am sure God touches the hearts of many through this.

You both have gone through much—and will continue to—but it is very obvious to me in listening to you (from the first of the year through July) that despite the pressure, your faith is increasing and your joy in the Lord is giving you strength to meet the challenge.

I know that this is a time of waiting on God that He might direct your future, and I know that God will bless you as you follow. For many years I had said to God, *Take hold of my coattail and try to keep up because I am going to do everything humanly possible.* Then when I failed, I would say, *Okay, God, You will have to take over for I can do nothing more.* It took me years to practice the art of letting God lead the way, for it is so easy to run off in your own strength. It was only when God had to pick up the pieces that I realized what I was doing.

A few years ago I heard a song which said: *If you can't take your burdens to the Lord, who in the world can you take them to?* And another stanza said: *If you can't trust God, who in the world can you trust?* Still another: *If He doesn't have the answers, who in the world does?* This song made me look at my life and see that I trusted God only for the hereafter and for the humanly impossible situations—in other words, I was limiting my faith . . . . As your total faith in God increases, so does your commitment to God increase. It also seems that as your commitment increases, so does your faith. In other words: one cannot be without the other.

I pray for God's richest blessings on you and your family, both spiritually and financially, as you walk God's pathways through life. God has looked after you well in giving you a pastor like Bill Chapman. I enjoyed him very much and I learned much from him. Many pastors encourage members to stand up and go—but all too often the pastor then sits down. Brother Chapman not only stood with you—he went, too.

Thank you for standing strong. God will use your new book in many different ways in the months to come. Some will see Christ Jesus for the first time; some will decide to really serve Him, and still others will get involved in politics. I hope all will have more love for the lost and try to win them.

A relative of yours in the family of Christ.

NANCY VANDERHIDER

The
Anita Bryant
Story

1
God Put a Flame in My Heart

Because of my love for Almighty God, because of my love for His Word, because of my love for my country, because of my love for my children, I took a stand—one that was not popular.

Never before had I taken a public stand on any political or controversial issue. As even our closest friends would tell you, I have chosen to live a very private life, even though as an entertainer, that is not always easy. But for the most part, my husband and manager, Bob Green, and I have sought to keep our home life as private as possible, deliberately avoiding that which might produce unfavorable public reaction. One reporter observed that I'd never been known before to raise my voice in anything but song. And he was right.

We were in the middle of a prayer time for revival in the Northwest Baptist Church in North Miami, Florida, which my family attends, where my husband is a deacon, and I teach Sunday school. For several years I, along with my husband and members of our church, had been praying that God would revive America, our community, and our families. I was praying for Bob and for our four children. Then it got down to the nitty-gritty when God said, "And how about you?" God drew a circle, figuratively speaking. I stepped inside, and He put a flame in my heart.

Word came to our pastor that there was a proposed ordinance in Miami which I thought, if passed, would give special privileges to homosexuals in areas of housing, public accommodation, and employment. As our pastor spoke, he noted the effect this ordinance would have on private and religious schools. I suddenly started to realize what he was saying. The thought of known homosexuals teaching my children especially in a religious school bothered me. It kept coming to my mind. I was into God's Word more deeply than ever before. All of a sudden I began to see that God doesn't tolerate a lot of things that people say they are willing to tolerate "in love." I couldn't say no to God when His Word is so plain.

During that revival period, under the faithful preaching of our pastor—the Reverend William Chapman, whom we all call Brother Bill—the Lord showed me that a part of my own personal revival would be to take more of an interest in what was going on around me in my community. All of this happened during the first week of January, 1977. Even in our wildest imaginings we could not have dreamed of what would come in succeeding months. The divine disturbance continued in my heart, and I knew God was telling me to go with others from our church to the Metro Commission hearing.

The deciding factor came when my husband pointed out to me that it was Ruth Shack, the wife of my booking agent, who had introduced the resolution which in my opinion would grant special privileges and open acceptance to homosexuals. I couldn't believe it. At first I couldn't accept it, and I questioned my husband, "Are you sure? Oh, she couldn't have done that! Oh, Bob, we supported her in her election campaign!"

But it was true. Dick Shack had been my agent for many years. When he asked me to tape a radio spot for his wife in her bid to run for the Dade County Metro Commission, I agreed, after talking it over with Bob. Ruth had some good ideas about different programs relating to ecology, helping the elderly, and other issues.

My mistake hit me full force when people from the church came to me and said, "I voted for Ruth Shack because you said to do it, and now look at the resolution she's introduced." When the realization of what they were saying dawned on me, it pierced my heart. I knew I had to do something of a public nature because of that earlier endorsement. More importantly though, I felt I had to take a stand against this ordinance because of the effect it would have on my children, and on all the children of Dade County.

I felt ashamed to think I had influenced people to vote for someone who later proposed this ordinance, even though at election time the issue had not come up. I wrestled with God and with conflicting emotions about my faith and my career. I was between a rock and a hard place, and I knew it. I was afraid of retaliation—of losing my life's work. But I've learned to obey God regardless of the consequences. I knew in my heart where I stood with God, and that was more important than anything else.

One Sunday morning about this time, I visited my son Bobby's Sunday-school class and heard Judi Wilson speak. I sensed she had a deep spiritual walk with the Lord. After I heard her speak I realized what love and compassion she had. I learned it was she who had first alerted our pastor to the proposed Metro ordinance. Judi was part of the convicting power of God which prompted me to speak out. When she called and said, "Anita, how can you as a Christian stand back and say nothing now!" I realized I had to take action.

I decided to begin by writing a personal letter to each of the nine Metro commissioners before the public hearing and vote which were scheduled for January 18. But before I wrote the letters, God impressed upon my heart the need to call Mrs. Shack and tell her what I intended to do and to express to her personally my feelings about the amendment she had proposed. I also wanted to know her reasons for making the proposal.

We talked for almost an hour. I was totally honest with her as I expressed my dismay at the stand she had taken. My efforts to persuade Ruth Shack failed. I reminded her of my lifelong dedication to a Christian and wholesome way of life and how Bob and I were committed to the moral upbringing of our children. I expressed the valid fears we now felt of widespread militant homosexuals' efforts to influence children to their abnormal way of life. But my arguments failed; Ruth Shack's view was unchanged. She believed the ordinance to be right, and I did not.

I told Brother Bill I would need his help in composing a letter with

Scripture to support my stand. I felt a compelling urgency to write individual letters to each of the commissioners. As it happened, our pastor was called to an emergency situation and never had time to help me. I also asked my husband for assistance, but he was on jury duty all that week. I felt so inadequate, but in between praying and crying and confessing to God my inadequacy and guilt, I got into His Word. I fell into bed at three in the morning, with all my thoughts and scriptural findings written down. I knew the Bible had some things to say on homosexuality. God didn't intend for me to rely upon anyone else. God always sees the end from the beginning, and He knew that in the long weeks ahead I would need to be able to quote those parts of Scripture with authority. The letter stated:

Dear Commissioner:

It has been brought to my attention that coming up on Tuesday, January 18, 1977, the Dade County Board of Commissioners will be considering an amendment to Chapter 11A of the Dade County Code, an ordinance prohibiting discrimination in the areas of housing, public accommodation and employment against persons based on their affectional or sexual preferences.

As a concerned mother of four children—ages 13 to 8 years—I am most definitely against this ordinance amendment. I have never condoned nor taught my children discrimination against anyone because of their race or religion, but if this ordinance amendment is allowed to become law, you will, in fact, be infringing upon my rights and discriminating against me as a citizen and a mother to teach my children and set examples and to point to others as examples of God's moral code as stated in the Holy Scriptures. Also, you would be discriminating against my children's right to grow up in a healthy, decent community that we're proud to be a part of. If Almighty God is not *the authority* on morality, then who is?

You may or may not believe in the authority of the Holy Scriptures, but this country was born because of that belief and the freedom to express that faith in Almighty God. What kind of community and nation would we have without God's morality?

Now I ask you, will the next ordinance be to protect the rights of prostitutes . . . . Where will this so-called *discrimination* end, when you are trying to legislate morality?

What a horrible example of marriage and the family unit you will be portraying to our children and for generations to come. "Nay, ye do wrong, and defraud . . . ." God said that in 1 Corinthians 6:8, and then in verse 9, He said: "Know ye not that the unrighteous shall not inherit the kingdom of God? Be not deceived: neither fornicators, nor idolaters, nor adulterers, nor effeminate, nor abusers of themselves with mankind," verse 10, "Nor thieves, nor covetous, nor drunkards, nor revilers, nor extortioners, shall inherit the kingdom of God."

Leviticus 20:13 says: "If a man also lie with mankind, as he lieth with a woman, both of them have committed an abomination: they shall surely be put to death; their blood shall be upon them."

Surely only God can judge mankind, certainly not I. But God is a Holy God and hates those kinds of sins, yet He loves us so much that He provided a sacrifice and covering for all of our sins. In John 3:16: "For God so loved the world, that he gave his only begotten Son, that whosoever believeth in him should not perish, but have everlasting life."

He also provided His Word, not only as a guide to eternal life, but to everyday life as well. He tells us to raise our children in the nurture and admonition of the Lord. He tells our children to obey their parents and uphold the law of the land! What confusion for our children this ordinance would create . . . .

In Jude 7, God warns us not to forget the cities of Sodom and Gomorrah and their neighboring towns, all full of lust of every kind, including lust of men for other men. Those cities

were destroyed by fire and continue to be a warning to us that
there is a hell in which sinners are punished.

I urge you with every ounce of my being to vote NO on the
amendment to ordinance Chapter 11A of the Dade County
Code.

                                    Respectfully,
                                    ANITA BRYANT GREEN

I really thought that expressions of concern like that letter would
make the difference. As the date for the hearing approached, I con-
sented to go on the air over several local radio talk-show programs.
These, along with publicity that was being generated by the media,
began to stir the interest of people in the community as they realized
the ordinance would affect private and religious schools in particular
and would have far-reaching implications in many other areas. Support was coming from unexpected sources. I was being introduced to
books and literature that helped reinforce my position not only from
a scriptural standpoint, but also from a factual and legal point of view.

During those weeks the sermons my pastor preached built up my
faith and confidence. I have never been the type of person who
enters into anything halfheartedly. Of course, God knows my nature,
and marvelously He saw to it that I received what I needed. The
messages were faith-building blocks forming a wall of protection
around me. I found many occasions to reflect on one sermon in
particular, taken from Jesus' words in Matthew 10. This passage
made me aware that I had to be cautious, and that in every step we
took, we had to be protective of our children and of each other as
Christians. But at the same time we were not to be vindictive toward
anyone or strike out at any individual person. We were to be harm-
less as doves, and we could claim the victory by looking to the Lord. I
knew where my power was coming from. Anita Bryant Green, in and
of herself, would have blown the whole thing.

I really did not want to go to the hearing, and I certainly didn't
want to have to get up and speak. I spent many agonizing hours

walking through our house, crying. Then I'd think: *If God is for me, how can anybody be against me?*

Shortly before the hearing, one of my twins, eight-and-a-half-year-old Barbara and I narrowly avoided a three-car collision as we were returning from a radio show. It was a wet night, and the cars involved were just ahead of us. Shaken, I pulled off the road and, with Barbara, offered a prayer of thanks. It was only by the grace of God that we didn't pile up, too.

Barbara took my hand and said, "Mama, if God can help us in a bad accident like that, can't He help you in the courtroom?" God reminded me through my child that not a hair of my head would be touched unless He allowed it and that I had nothing to fear. When I returned home, I told Bob that if God wanted me to speak at the hearing, I wouldn't be afraid anymore.

2
The Battle for Miami

The battle lines were drawn in Miami on that memorable cold January morning. The foot soldiers were housewives and mothers, religious and civic leaders in opposition to a well-organized, highly financed, and politically militant group of homosexual activists.

We emerged at the scene of the controversy as an unorganized but deeply concerned and committed group of parents and citizens upon whom had been foisted an ordinance which was against everything we believed in and stood for. We had neither marshaled our defenses, nor had we developed a strategy as the leaders of the militant homosexual movement had obviously done. We had done our homework: We did know why we were there, but there was nothing political or militant in our motives. Most of us had never seen each other before, and our first introductions were at the courthouse.

As the nation was to see in succeeding weeks, our stand brought death threats, harassment, heartache, distortions of statements by the media, tremendous pressures, disruption of our private lives, and a host of problems we had not envisioned when we took our stand. For me, in addition to all of the above, it brought job discrimination and the loss of a lifelong dream of having a television show of my own. We were cast as bigots, haters, discriminators, and deniers of basic human rights. And all of this happened because we were sincerely concerned for our children and our community.

I felt strong, confident, and at peace. I had carefully studied the wording of the amendment. I knew the Scriptures. My own personal preparation for the confrontation was complete. People were praying. We had prayed, and even while we were in that hearing, the

Lord was reading my heart and hearing the cries welling up from deep within me. I knew God's hand was upon us.

The local "gay" activists were there with those who had joined them in their defense of the ordinance. Under the banner of the Dade County Coalition for the Humanistic Rights of Gays, they flexed their political muscles. While much of the media and sympathizers to the homosexuals were shouting about discrimination, the spokesman for the local group admitted at the hearing that homosexuals as individuals *are* able to obtain housing, employment, and education without discrimination in Dade County. "We are there now and what we want to do is tell you where we're at," their avowed leader said.

"If there is no discrimination, then there is no need for this ordinance," said Mayor Steve Clark.

We outnumbered the opposition by eight to one at the hearing, even though they brought in some speakers from out of state. Homosexuals in Dade County had made a discovery during the local elections the preceding year—they discovered they had political clout. Dade County became another testing ground for them in their continuing nationwide efforts to gain so-called rights and life-style approval. This was to be proved in the months ahead as political organizers from around the country joined them in launching a full-fledged crusade.

Proponents of the ordinance framed the issue as civil rights versus bigotry. Nothing could have been further from the truth. At the hearing, the leaders of the homosexual movement had their say first. When it came time for those of us who opposed the ordinance to speak, some very articulate religious and civic leaders in the community presented views which we felt validated our stand and would compel the Metro Commission to reverse its original vote.

Reverend Charles Couey from South Dade Baptist Church was the first man called on to speak for our side. There was an immediately noticeable hush throughout the room as this man of God stood with only the Word of God in his hands and, without expounding or explaining the Scripture in any way, read from the first chapter of Romans.

Professing themselves to be wise, they became fools. And changed the glory of the uncorruptible God into an image made like to corruptible man, and to birds, and fourfooted beasts, and creeping things. Wherefore God also gave them up to uncleanness, through the lusts of their own hearts, to dishonour their own bodies between themselves: Who changed the truth of God into a lie, and worshipped and served the creature more than the Creator, who is blessed for ever. Amen.

For this cause God gave them up unto vile affections: for even their women did change the natural use into that which is against nature: And likewise also the men, leaving the natural use of the woman, burned in their lust one toward another; men with men working that which is unseemly, and receiving in themselves that recompence of their error which was meet.

And even as they did not like to retain God in their knowledge, God gave them over to a reprobate mind, to do those things which are not convenient; Being filled with all unrighteousness, fornication, wickedness, covetousness, maliciousness; full of envy, murder, debate, deceit, malignity; whisperers, Backbiters, haters of God, despiteful, proud, boasters, inventors of evil things, disobedient to parents, Without understanding, covenantbreakers, without natural affection, implacable, unmerciful: Who knowing the judgment of God, that they which commit such things are worthy of death, not only do the same, but have pleasure in them that do them.

Romans 1:22–32

The Roman Catholic Church, through its attorney, prominent Miamian Joseph Fitzgerald, said the ordinance would permit known practicing homosexuals to teach in private church schools and to act as role models for their pupils, showing that homosexuality is an acceptable and respectable alternative to the life-style of the children's parents. This, he said, would be directly counter to teachings of the Catholic Church. Later, Archbishop Coleman Carroll, prestigious leader of South Florida's heavy Catholic population and its fifty-six schools, said the Church would refuse to obey the law and would oppose it vigorously in the courts.

These comments were particularly significant in view of the fact that, by a peculiarity of the Dade County charter, the Metro Commission has no authority over the large public-school population of the county, the sixth largest in the nation. The new homosexual license would have applied solely to private and religious schools. In Dade County there are more that a hundred such schools: Jewish, Protestant, secular, and Catholic.

Robert M. Brake, a Coral Gables city commissioner and a former Metro Commissioner, said the ordinance was a bad law and maintained that homosexuals were already granted all rights against discrimination under existing federal laws. This effort, he said, was a carefully disguised attempt to break down further the moral fabric of society. He said the law would give these people special privileges that would only be to the detriment of society in general and children in particular.

Alvin Dark, former manager of the champion Oakland A's and now manager of the San Diego Padres, simply opened his Bible and gave the plan of salvation for *any* sinner.

When it was my turn to speak, I addressed the mayor and members of the commission with these words:

> I come here today with no prejudice in my heart, no hate, no anger, or judgment against my fellowman. But I do come with a deep burden for my country, my community, and my children's well-being.
>
> The commissioners have already received my letter and know full well my stand as a Christian, and I make no apologies for that.
>
> I'm speaking to you today not as an entertainer who has worked with homosexuals all my life—and I have never discriminated against them; I have a policy of live and let live as long as they do not discriminate against me. But I am a wife and a mother, and I especially address you today as a mother. I have a God-given right to be jealous of the

moral environment for my children.

I remind you that the God who made us could have made us like the sea turtle who comes in the dark of night and buries her eggs in the sand and never cares about her children again. But God created us so our children would be dependent upon us as their parents for their lives. And I, for one, will do everything I can as a citizen, as a Christian, and especially as a mother to insure that they have the right to a healthy and morally good life.

The cry of work discrimination has been the key that has unlocked the door of freedom to *legitimate* minority groups; now, it is time to recognize the rights of the overwhelming majority of Dade County who are being discriminated against because they have the right to say no. Just when did the word *discrimination* start meaning "I can't say no"? The people of Dade County can't say no now in the areas of housing, employment, and education. But I can, and I do say no to a very serious moral issue that would violate my rights and the rights of all decent and morally upstanding citizens, regardless of their race or religion.

We urge the Dade County Commissioners to act responsibly for the vast majority of their constituents . . . .

Because we were not organized, Orthodox Rabbi Phineas Weberman did not get to speak, but he did present his statement to the commissioners afterwards. He said his five-thousand-year-old religion had always condemned homosexuality as unnatural, unproductive, sinful, and a flagrant violation of God's laws and the laws of the vast majority of mankind in all ages.

And there were others who spoke out against the ordinance that day. We all agreed that we were opposed to their demands for what they considered a basic "right" and the affirmation by society that what they were doing was right. But our voices were united in protest. It was not solely a religious issue, as our opponents kept insisting; it was a moral issue on which society has a right to make its own contrary judgment.

Of course we were naive enough to think our presence and testimony were going to sway the commissioners. Had it been an actual court trial, the case would have been thrown out because the only reason for proposing the amendment was to show discrimination where there was none.

Immediately after hearing arguments from both sides, the commission voted. The measure was passed by a five-to-three vote, setting up what had to be an inevitable future confrontation. The fight was not over. The commission majority included Ruth Shack, Bill Oliver, James Redford, Beverly Phillips, and Harvey Ruvin. Opponents included Metro Mayor Steve Clark and Commissioners Clara Oesterle and Neal Adams. Barry Schreiber was absent because of illness.

I was visibly stunned, as were the others. I couldn't believe it. I was devastated. I sat there, and I heard the result of the vote, and I thought. *This is a free country, and if we present our case and we're right and if it's proven, then we should win it.*

That's what shocked me so badly—to think we live in a country where freedom and right are supposed to reign, a country that boasts "In God we trust" and has such a rich spiritual heritage; yet where internal decadence is all too evident, where the Word of God and the voice of the majority is sometimes not heeded at all. Has it come to this: that we are a society that in fact does glorify aberrant behavior and oppresses the rights of the majority on a moral issue? I was not the only one in the room that day who was thoroughly disillusioned.

Suddenly the TV cameras started rolling and zeroing in. "Who's your leader?"; "How do you feel?"; "Are you disappointed?"

"Yes," I said, "I'm disappointed, and I'm shaken, but the flame that God put in my heart is becoming a torch. It will not be quenched. We have just begun to fight."

I was aflame with indignation. The Bible calls it "righteous anger."

Immediately following the vote, those of us who were in opposition met. There was a mixture of outrage and deep sadness. Some of us felt numb. Robert Brake stepped up and introduced himself. He said we needed to form an organized effort to defeat this ordinance by petition and referendum. We would need an organization. His next question was: "Would you head it up, Anita, as chairman?"

I turned to my husband, who was as outraged and disturbed as I, and we conferred. The answer, of course, had to be yes. There could be no turning back now. We still did not know, however, the repercussions that would be felt because of all this. I was quoted in the papers as saying, "Even if my livelihood is stripped away from me, I will not be moved. I'd rather have the love of God and be making this a better place to live for my children and other children." And I meant it. With all my heart I meant it then, and I mean it now.

I would give my life, if necessary, to protect my children. I'm concerned about giving them the right food and meeting all their physical needs, but if I let up on their spiritual welfare, what good is it?

The media misquoted me, saying that I called homosexuals *garbage*. That was *not* what I said. As I talked about our concern for the health and diet of our children and other people's children, I said, "If they are exposed to homosexuality, I might as well feed them garbage." I think there is a difference, but I leave it to the reader to interpret as you wish—we did not resort to name-calling at any time during the campaign in Miami.

Criticism from the media was an eye-opener for me. We were quoted and misquoted time after time. A case in point is an interview I had with the religion editor of the Orlando *Sentinel-Star*. I quoted the familiar 1 Corinthians 6:9 passage which lists the "unrighteous [who] shall not inherit the kingdom of God." I said to her that murderers, drunkards, thieves, homosexuals, and *all* who have not turned from their sin are included as needing to be repentant. The headline in the paper read: ANITA BRYANT CALLS HOMOSEXUALS MURDERERS!

There were all kinds of lies and distortions including one in particular which concerned a bumper sticker which allegedly said: KILL A QUEER FOR CHRIST. May the Lord strike me dead if I or any member of Save Our Children had anything to do with such a supposed bumper sticker. To this date I have yet to find one person who has even seen such a sticker. This happened over and over again.

But we stood strong in our defense against what we saw as encroaching moral decay in America, and in our own city and county in particular. Hundreds of newspaper and magazine clippings came our way; the comments ranged from my being accused of sounding a homophobic pitch to being called "a courageous woman."

As we stood outside the courtroom chambers, we knew we had to face this moral crisis. Later on I knew, from information that had been sent to me, that in California this same kind of battle had been fought and all but lost due to the apathy of the public. With the help of our local religious and civic leaders, I sensed that we as wives and mothers had to march out of our living rooms and fight for the repeal of this ordinance. I joined with Judi Wilson and others who emphasized, "This is not a hate campaign. We're motivated because we love our children, our nation, and our country. And we have love and concern for homosexuals, too."

3

A Space to Repent

As we left the hearing, Brother Bill said, "Come on over to the house, and we'll just talk. Peggy makes the best banana sandwiches!"

I was still somewhat in a state of shock. At the time I didn't exactly appreciate, and certainly didn't understand, that bit of pastoral psychology. I remember thinking: *Banana sandwiches! He must be kidding. Who would eat a banana sandwich!*

"Brother Bill," I asked, "are you sure God will forgive me for my sin of ignorance and for not being more aware of the issues and for having my head in the sand and being so apathetic?"

"Anita," he patiently replied, "you know your sins are covered by the blood of Christ so long as you confess them. My dear, you will not be held accountable."

We sat in the pleasant kitchen of the Chapmans', and I wept. Tears, I am convinced, are a gift of God and are part of a healing process we go through when we are wounded, particularly when we are wounded for His sake.

"It's all over," I remember saying, "and I'm so down."

As we drank glasses of milk and ate our banana sandwiches, the pastor started whistling "Victory in Jesus."

"I'm down," I said, thinking aloud, "but not out!"

Brother Bill stopped whistling and looked at us and said, "You know what it is?" He paused, noticing that we were finally relaxing. "God has given us *a space to repent.*"

"How do you know that?" I asked him.

"Revelation, chapter 2, verse 21. The writer had been describing the wicked prophetess Jezebel, and then he says: 'And I gave her space to repent of her fornication; and she repented not.' Remember, the Book of Revelation is a book of prophecy. America is being given time—a space to repent."

"Explain yourself," I urged.

"A 'space to repent' is more than a phrase found in the Bible. It is a truth proven in biblical and secular history. In God's marvelous grace there is always the provision for a space to repent. This is so in a nation's life as well as in an individual's life. It is my strong belief that God in His grace is giving America this opportunity now," he explained.

"But what if a nation or an individual doesn't heed?" I asked.

"After the space to repent comes the judgment and wrath of God. This was so in such classic Bible examples as Noah and his generation, and Lot in Sodom and Gomorrah. It's terribly sad, but so many people misinterpret the grace of God in granting this space to repent before His judgment. The Bible says in Ecclesiastes 8, verse 11: 'Because sentence against an evil work is not executed speedily, therefore the heart of the sons of men is fully set in them to do evil.' In other words, many say we sin and judgment doesn't take place immediately, therefore, we 'get away with' sinning. Not so! Judgment *will* follow. We have the clear teaching of the Bible which tells us over and over again that 'we shall all stand before the judgment seat of Christ.' " (*See* Romans 14:10.)

"What will America do with her space to repent?" I asked my pastor.

"One of two things will come to pass, Anita," he replied. "There will be revival or ruin. Only God knows!"

What an individual does with God and the Bible has everything to do with his character and life-style. Historically, the Church has been society's conscience and has provided its moral and spiritual leadership. But when the Church and believers fail to uphold the biblical standards or righteousness, then we cease to be the Church of Jesus Christ. The secular world defines morality on the basis of acceptable standards it has erected, and they change like the wind. But God's revealed truth is the *only* standard the Christian Church can accept. There are those who say, "God is love," and, "We are all God's children," failing to realize you cannot separate God's love from His righteousness.

God's love is not inconsistent with His holiness and His opposition to sin. The Bible reveals Jesus as the human face of God. On earth, Jesus dealt with sin whenever and wherever He saw it. When He met the woman taken in adultery, who the townspeople considered a notorious sinner, He forgave her. But He did something else that many people conveniently overlook: He told her, ". . . go, and sin no more" (John 8:11).

If Jesus had met a homosexual that day, He would have forgiven his sin as well. But in His next breath, Jesus would have said the same thing to the homosexual that He said to the adulterous woman. Jesus was upholding His Father's standard of righteousness; He came to fulfill the law, not to abolish it. Throughout the Gospels, Jesus emphasized the seriousness of sin and the consequences of disobedience. Jesus' love for sinners compelled Him to deal with the sin in their lives—He forgave it.

The Church of Jesus Christ does sinners no favor when it comforts them in their sins—homosexuality included. The weaknesses of man's flesh are to be confronted with God's demands for right living. There is a way out of the sin dilemma: God has provided all the help, hope, and love a person needs to overcome his or her sin problem. We are all sinners who need God's forgiveness and mercy. Some of us have discovered that God is true to His Word: He can be trusted to do what He says. However, we—as Christians—are also called to forgive as we have been forgiven (see Matthew 6:12; Luke 6:37).

Those of us who came to the hearing in Miami were being true to God's directives. He still chooses to use people to carry forth His message today. The Church and Christians must accept their share of the responsibility for the world's moral landslide. We have not always responded as we should.

Many denominations are unwilling to take a firm biblical stand on the homosexual issue. This is reflected in some of the rulings and statements handed down from their conferences. One of the finest position papers we received came from the Reverend Jerry R. Kirk of the College Hill Presbyterian Church of Cincinnati, Ohio. It is his belief that the Church is at a crossroads; God has called us to costly grace and a godly life. We are to be accountable to Him and to one another. The question we now face is whether we will call one another to be accountable.

Kirk expressed great concern that so many, even within the Church, are redefining the Bible's teachings on morality. They are even going so far as to redefine repentance and forgiveness. Kirk asks the questions: If the roots of morality are pulled from the biblical revelation, what is the meaning of salvation? And what basis would the Church have for being society's conscience and providing its moral and spiritual leadership? In addition, if God's clear teaching concerning morality can be so totally redefined, on what basis can we believe anything in Scripture? Kirk states that we have a crisis of faith and we are caving in to the messages and pressures of the secular world. He points out, as so many of us have been doing, that, historically, these have always led to disaster.

Kirk further points out that we are in danger of being ashamed of what Jesus taught and the righteousness for which He stood. We are in danger of losing our moral leadership and prophetic voice because of shallow thinking, a sentimental definition of love, and the breakdown of marital fidelity and moral integrity even among many of our own leaders and members. I agree wholeheartedly with this minister who believes we are in danger of being led by people who have already capitulated to the rampant and militant paganism and immorality surrounding us, and are even now in the process of seeking the Church's support for establishing a rational basis for their own rationalizations. In the process they are using well-meaning and loving persons who are not knowledgeable of Scripture, however, nor committed to its authority.

Dade County became the focal point for the homosexual issue, but as everyone has now come to realize, it is hardly a local issue! Many religious leaders phoned, sent telegrams, and wrote to me, expressing their belief that seldom in recent years has the Church faced an issue which could so radically divide and alienate Christian brothers and sisters, congregations as a whole, and denominational structures from the grass roots.

"Anyone who loves the Church must be acutely aware that we face issues and answers which will shake the Church to its foundations," Kirk writes. "But our love for unity and peace must not blind us to the mandate for purity. Jesus is no less concerned for purity of the Church . . . . Any genuine pastoral concern must include the commitment to seeking unity and purity."

Communicare magazine, published by Miami Christian College, devoted almost an entire issue to the subject "The Gospel and the Gay." When it came time to write my book, Dr. Kenneth O. Gangel, president of the college, opened up his files and gave me access to all of the research material that had been used in the preparation of that issue of the magazine. That magazine, as much as anything, was invaluable to me in giving me a better understanding of the entire homosexual scene as it confronts us.

Dr. Gangel writes:

> The present status of gay activism makes it imperative that thinking Christians really understand the situation on the national scene . . . .
>
> Evangelical Christians need to be alert to the implications of this gay force in their communities, their churches, and their nation. But most of all, they need to understand the underlying biblical and theological assumptions which have always made the church of Jesus Christ, though not always in an intelligent and loving way, clearly and unequivocably condemn homosexuality. The response of the real Christian on the issue of homosexuality should not be an emotional trauma toward the repulsion and stigma attached to the movement and its adherents. It should rather be a clear exposition of what the Bible has to say on the subject, with redemptive goals which have clear ramifications in society and the church.

We have found that when you stick your neck out on controversial issues, you must pay a price. That, of course, explains in part why our nation has been so flooded with filth in recent years. There have not been enough people willing to stick their necks out and say yes to

God and His absolute standards of truth, ethics, and morality. The very thing that happened to us in Miami is feared by many citizens of this land. Rather than face those consequences, they have chosen to remain silent while the more vocal radical groups have all but taken over in high places, both locally and nationally. This explains also why certain Christian leaders refused to stand up and be counted in this issue.

What would have happened if we had lost the vote in Dade County? What if the homosexuals had won? Would the Christians of this country have protested? Would they have assaulted the media with their ads and insistence on equal time on the air? Would you have paraded, marched, and done more? Would the "straights" have instituted boycotts as advocated by the pro-ERA people in this nation? Would those who call themselves the godly of this country have demonstrated by economic sanction? Would those who claim to be the followers of Christ have shown the same zeal and dedication as those who are the followers of the "gay" leaders?

These are questions I have found myself asking as I write this book. This reluctance on the part of so many, to say an out and out yes to God and no to sin and its accompanying evil, has brought our present generation to its sorry state. We were not opposing an individual's right to be treated with equality and fairness, but we did rise in opposition to the misleading demand of so-called civil rights for homosexuals who are not a legitimate oppressed minority with the same claims and rights as, say, Chicanos or blacks.

The Black Muslim publication *Muhammad Speaks* reported: HOMOSEXUALS DEMAND SPECIAL RIGHTS. The Honorable Eman Wallis D. Muhammad, spiritual leader, said, "Homosexuals already have the same rights as other members of society under the law. The trouble with our world is that we have lost contact with common sense." In the same article, Dr. Bobby Wright, director of Chicago's Garfield Park Comprehensive Mental Health Center, said, "They [homosexuals] have tried to confuse the black community by persuading the black community that all forms of discrimination are equated with the struggle. The homosexuals came in on the civil-rights movement, attached themselves to it, and tried to take it over to the point of equating civil rights with homosexual rights. It is a political weapon that we have to be very careful not to become involved in."

In the *New Pittsburgh Courier,* black columnist Nathaniel Clay proclaimed, "Blacks and Gays: An Odious Comparison." In the article, he quoted Thedford Johnson, a black Miami minister who said, "When you're black it sticks. You're segregated for the way you look. No one has to know what these people ["gays"] are unless they want it [known]." The we-are-birds-of-a-feather appeal to the blacks by the homosexuals was soundly rejected.

The attempt by homosexuals to label this a civil-rights issue was nothing but camouflage. If we as a nation eventually come to the place where this is sanctioned as a legitimate civil-rights issue, then what is to stop the adulterer from claiming "adulterer rights," the murderer from shouting "murderer rights," the thief to claim "extortioner rights," and a rebellious young person to insist on "rebellious-child rights"?

The misunderstanding that exists in the minds of so many was seen, for instance, when actress Liv Ullman appeared on the "Good Morning America" show. David Hartman introduced her, and Sandy Hill asked: "Liv, why do you feel so strongly about speaking out against Anita Bryant and her cause?"

Liv said, "Because it's a violation of human rights, civil rights, and it doesn't only concern gay people, it concerns everybody, who sooner or later in life might belong to a group that will be discriminated [against] . . . ."

That view was shared, as was to be expected, by others in the entertainment field such as composer Paul Williams, singer Jaye P. Morgan, actresses Jane Fonda, Martha Raye, Shirley MacLaine, and Phyllis Diller, actors Ed Asner (who played newsman Lou Grant in the "Mary Tyler Moore" series) and Peter Lawford, entertainer Florence Henderson, and others. My stand was most persistently attacked by Johnny Carson.

Carson's monologues were described by Tom Shales, writing in the Washington *Post,* as "growing increasingly audacious and topical" particularly as they concerned my stand. He wrote:

The image of Bryant that emerges from the Carson monologues—repeatedly to the cheers and laughter of, one presumes, a largely heterosexual studio audience—is that of a prudish, self-righteous fanatic. Was the New York blackout an "act of God"? No, said Carson, because "Anita Bryant would never have given Him time off."

Tom Shales explains Carson's tone as "not hostile, but clearly derisive," and he predicted, "Bryant jokes will be particularly plentiful on the new fall comedy shows coming up." The premiere performance of the new "Laugh In" show was another prime example of the show-biz conspiracy to ridicule and discredit me. By this time in the campaign, it had become obvious to me that very few people in the entertainment industry are willing to search for, and stand up and speak out on, the side of decency.

There are those who wonder how I feel about bearing the brunt of such jokes. I shall let the apostle Paul tell you how I feel:

> What a wonderful God we have—he is the Father of our Lord Jesus Christ, the source of every mercy, and the one who so wonderfully comforts and strengthens us in our hardships and trials. And why does he do this? So that when others are troubled, needing our sympathy and encouragement, we can pass on to them this same help and comfort God has given us. You can be sure that the more we undergo sufferings for Christ, the more he will shower us with his comfort and encouragement. We are in deep trouble . . . . But in our trouble God had comforted us—and this, too, to help you: to show you from our personal experience how God will tenderly comfort you when you undergo . . . sufferings. *He will give you the strength to endure.*
> 2 Corinthians 1:3–7 LB

> . . . But who is adequate for such a task as this? Only those who, like ourselves, are men of integrity, sent by God, speaking with Christ's power, with God's eye upon us . . . .
> 2 Corinthians 2:16, 17 LB

My heart's longing is to see the people of this country who claim to be truly born again rise in defense of the truth of God's Word. We cannot defeat sin and all that is going on in this country if, as a Southern Baptist, Presbyterian, Reformed, Lutheran, Methodist, Episcopalian, Orthodox, Catholic, fundamentalist, charismatic, evangelical—whatever you name yourself—we are differing among ourselves. We need to put our differences aside on major issues that confront us which attempt to spoil the family unit. We need to let the world see that they—those who, like the militant homosexuals, laugh in the face of sin—are the offenders; we, the morally concerned citizens, are the defenders. This has been reversed by the media largely through the efforts of the militant-homosexual community which knows how to get to the decision-making media people and to our representatives in government both local and federal. What are you personally doing to influence the media and our government? What is your church, your denomination, doing?

The militant homosexuals in this country and their sympathizers don't realize the extent of my Christian convictions. They don't comprehend what my commitment to Christ really means.

They think that my priorities are where their priorities are—in money, careers, power, doing what makes one feel good. It is not even within their realm of thinking that someone would sacrifice her career to stand for what she believes. But this I have been willing to do. The "gay" activists cannot comprehend that we have been the happiest in our lives since all this began, because we know we are doing what God has asked us to do. There is no satisfaction that equals it. The Lord and our family come first. This is what, in the idiom of the world, "turns us on." We have not been destroyed because of this; we have been strengthened. Through it all I was working as if everything depended on me, but I was praying, knowing everything depended on God. And it did! And it does! And He does not let down those who trust and obey Him.

The Bible may be an antiquated book to many, but for the believer it is actually God speaking. God says there are some things that are evil and some things that are good. That's simple enough for even a child to understand. Certain things are right; other things are wrong. But they are right or wrong because God says so. We are right when we do God's will; we are wrong when we do not.

A child cannot be expected to act responsibly at all times, because he is immature. He is not yet able to sort things out and choose wisely. Responsibility must be assumed for the child in many instances. That is our role as parents. That is why the concerned citizens and aroused parents reacted as they did to the Dade County ordinance.

There are homosexual adults who are living irresponsibly, who in the name of "human rights" seek social rights that in reality only give them license for perversion and the flaunting of their deviant ways. To allow this to continue is only an indication that rather than being a great society, we are a sick society.

Justice is delayed and far too often bypassed on the basis of legal technicalities in order to preserve an individual's "rights," but *right* has been made a mockery.

To talk about the "rights" of someone who has chosen to rebel against responsible living is nonsense. It is simply not true that all human beings have the same rights. Some human beings throw away their rights by throwing away their responsibilities when we no longer dare to say no and prove we mean it by enforcing it. The power of the law is an empty gesture. All end up turning their backs on crime and/or that which would thrust them into an unpopular stance with the powerful makers of public opinion—the media.

Someone wrote to me that it is very regretful that the Church and Christians are often the last to express concern about unhealthy sexual attitudes in America. I agreed, and knew that taking a stand would call for intellectual integrity as well as conviction. I prayed we would possess both.

When principles are at stake, get involved. There can be no such thing as neutrality in the things of God. In our Judeo-Christian heritage, God has His prophets in every age who, for the most part, make enemies and become the target for much hatred. Elijah wasn't exactly popular with the people when he stood up and declared: "How long halt ye between two opinions? if the LORD be God, follow him: but if Baal, then follow him. And the people answered him not a word" (1 Kings 18:21).

Joshua, a great leader and successor of Moses, a man who helped change the course of the land of Israel, urged the people to make a decision and become involved. ". . . choose you this day who ye will serve . . . but as for me and my house, we will serve the LORD" (Joshua 24:15).

The First Alliance Church in Miami sent a copy of their church bulletin in which it was stated:

> Neutrality is our worst enemy. Two major mistakes can be made during a lifetime. One is to make the wrong decision and the other is to make no decision. Some wish to be neither fish nor fowl. They just float along with the tide. To take sides means to have enemies and friends. To not take sides means a lack of respect from all sides. Neutrality is not in the vocabulary of a Christian. You are for everything God is. You are against everything He declares displeasure with in His Word.

The writer of Proverbs wrote: "Righteousness exalteth a nation: but sin is a reproach to any people" (Proverbs 14:34).

We left the Chapman home following the hearing more determined than ever to stand on the side of righteousness, and determined to show the American people that God has given us "a space to repent."

4

The Save Our Children Movement

It was my husband, Bob, who came up with the name Save Our Children, Inc. to identify those of us who were rallying to defeat the local ordinance by petition and referendum. He spent a day prior to our first meeting praying for God's guidance and mapping out campaign strategy.

I immediately got to work telephoning all the people we had met in the courtroom and others whose names were given to us. In addition my pastor gave us the names of synagogue leaders and church pastors who should be called. I stayed up until midnight each night for a week making calls and working with Bob on plans for the first Save Our Children meeting. (The name of the organization is being changed.) On the first Wednesday after the hearing, a steering committee met in our home.

Rabbi Phineas Weberman opened that meeting with prayer. Bob Brake explained the wording of the petitions and how we were to go about getting them signed. The group approved the name Save Our Children, Inc., and we were on our way. Officers were elected and that's how I became the official president that day. Rev. William Chapman, Rabbi Weberman, Alvin Dark, Magaly Llaguno, and others were asked to serve as vice presidents. Bob Brake became secretary, and my husband, treasurer.

We were booked for a January 28 appearance on the popular Christian television talk show "The PTL Club." Host Jim Bakker asked, "Does it present problems being a Christian and an entertainer at the same time?" It was a loaded question at that juncture in our lives! Newspapers had picked up the battle waging in Miami and so had television and radio. We were beginning to feel the flak. We answered that at times it does indeed present *real big problems*.

I explained to the audience that when you are in show business, people say there are two things you shouldn't do: talk about religion or politics, and get involved in either one. Our goal has always been to put God first. I am never ashamed of the Gospel and never apologize for speaking about Jesus Christ.

Three weeks later, we were on "The PTL Club" again. Jim Bakker commended the Florida Citrus Commission for recognizing my right to speak out as a private citizen. So-called "gay rights" leaders were calling our efforts bigoted and fanatical. And they tried—unsuccessfully—to pressure the Florida Citrus Commission, for which I had been advertising orange juice since 1968, into taking my ads off the air. There was also talk of a nationwide boycott of Florida citrus products. It was this to which Jim Bakker referred. That was in mid-February when the first national boycott was announced. We have been unable to keep up with all the national boycotts since then but they have all been unsuccessful, and Florida orange juice is selling better than ever!

"The PTL Club" viewers heard me state: "We are in the middle of a battle that the Lord opened my eyes to . . . . Homosexuals want to come out of the closet. We are not against homosexuals, but we are against the act . . . . When I first heard about what they were attempting to do in Dade County, the Lord took hold of my heart . . . . What we are standing up against is militant homosexuals who are highly financed, highly organized, and who were able to ramrod the amendment through in our city . . . .

"When society deliberately rejects God, the Bible tells us God will give them up to uncleanness," I continued. "We need today to listen to the voice of history, for it confirms the warnings in God's Word. We know that the once-powerful Roman Empire gradually rotted from within and fell to barbarian invaders; just so, our civilization is headed for destruction unless we change our present course.

"We felt that we had to take a stand along with other concerned Miamians. We are faced with an aggressive social epidemic in this country, but, praise God, I do believe in the decency of the American people, and I believe this downward trend can be reversed . . . ."

My husband was equally vocal on "The PTL Club" as he brought up the fact that many leaders of the ERA (Equal Rights Amendment) and the NOW (National Organization for Women) support the militant homosexuals and their demands for special privileges. The more we got involved with the campaign, the more we could see the far-reaching implication of this nationwide.

On February 24 we appeared on the popular Christian talk show "The 700 Club." Pat Robertson, the well-respected host, encouraged us to tell about what was happening in Dade County.

"We believe in the Word of God, and there it says that homosexuality is an abomination . . . . Homosexual acts are illegal under Florida law and the laws of most states. The Metro Commission, nevertheless, chose to ignore the spirit of our laws and caved in to the small, vocal group of militant homosexuals . . . . We have formed an organization . . . and we are working toward a referendum so the public can decide."

We received an avalanche of mail after "The 700 Club" and "The PTL Club" appearances. Jim Bakker referred to the initial program as being "the bombshell that exploded over America."

Following our appearances on these programs, their hosts received threats, saying that if we were to discuss the homosexual issue again on their programs, the local station would pull the plug out, as would other stations throughout the nation. In New York, as well as in Los Angeles, "The 700 Club" was actually pulled off the air.

But the letters that came to us were a continuing source of encouragement. There were letters from wives and mothers, churches, religious organizations, civic groups, congressmen and other leaders in government, businessmen, women's and men's clubs (both religious and civic), and from well-known religious leaders. People from every walk of life and from all age groups responded.

An Orthodox bishop from the South reminded me of a quotation by the eighteenth-century British statesman, Edmund Burke, who said: "All that is necessary for the triumph of evil is that good men do nothing."

But "The PTL Club" and "The 700 Club" appearances came, providentially we believe, at just the right time to help focus the truth on *our* side of the issue, since the opposition had called a press conference to boycott Florida orange juice and had brought nation-wide attention on the Dade County homosexual issue. As the enormity of all this began to dawn upon us, there were times when we were full of fear and trembling because of the step we had taken. Then the letters and telegrams lifted us up. We needed that love and edification from God's people.

Once back home we had to plunge into the activities of Save Our Children, Inc. Another meeting had been called, and this time we met at a warehouse that would accommodate the huge crowd we expected.

In our absence, Bob Brake had gone before the Metro Commission to get approval of initiative petitions to force the commission to either reverse its vote or to place the question on a referendum ballot. The petitions had to be numbered by the voter-registration office before we could distribute them to church, club, and organization representatives.

We were greatly encouraged to learn that the Dade County Federation of Women's Clubs, an organization of fifty clubs with approximately ten thousand members, had gone on record in opposition to the amendment. They had sent us a copy of their letter to Mayor Steve Clark and the commissioners. That same organization sent a similar letter to the Florida Citrus Commission and the First Federal Savings & Loan Association of Miami (for whom I also do TV commercials and who had also been threatened with boycott by "gay" activists).

My husband, Bob, opened his heart to the crowd which had assembled. He expressed what was probably on everyone's heart, "It appears that the homosexuals want to make Miami a Mecca for sin, but we don't want that to happen. If it does, we are going to be held accountable for it also; so it just means we are all going to have to put our shoulders to the wheel. Anita just mentioned that this is like Noah's ark. Aren't you glad you're on board?"

Monsignor Peter Reilly, pastor of Miami's Church of the Little Flower and official representative of Archbishop Carroll, prayed a prayer that was moving in its simplicity and had a motivating impact:

With compassion in our hearts for all of our fellow men and women caught in the web of error . . . .

With full respect for everyone's basic human rights, we initiate a campaign to protect our children from any influence that would mar their moral lives.

Guide us, Lord, that we may be inspired by a spirit of friendship and justice in all our actions. Amen.

I shared the burden that was on my heart: "It was announced in the local papers that we came into the courtroom as a very highly organized group and that we came in anger and hate. I resented that kind of judgment. But I know my own heart, it was not out of hate, it was out of love—not only love for God's commandments and His Word, but love for my children and yours. Yes, and love for all sinners—even homosexuals.

"After the courtroom appearance, most of us met for the first time, representing different segments of society. People were there just because of their concern for the morals of Dade County, and people were there because they loved God—the Catholics, the Jews, and the Protestants. We decided we needed to form an organization. A few days later we met at our home and that's how Save Our Children started. That is the basic foundation of what we are all about and why we are here today . . . .

"On the day of the hearing a friend said, 'Anita, I want to share the devotional message from *Streams in the Desert* for today.' I went through much fear and trepidation before making that courtroom appearance, but after hearing that devotion I felt calm and assured of God's presence going before us. I've read it every day since then, and now I want to read it to you."

Now thanks be unto God, which always causeth us to triumph in Christ.

2 Corinthians 2:14

God gets His greatest victories out of apparent defeats. Very often the enemy seems to triumph for a little, and God lets it be so; but then He comes in and upsets all the work of the enemy, overthrows the apparent victory, and as the Bible says, "turns the way of the wicked upside down." Thus He gives a great deal larger victory than we would have known if He had not allowed the enemy, seemingly, to triumph in the first place . . . .

The story of the three Hebrew children being cast into the fiery furnace is a familiar one. Here was an apparent victory for the enemy. It *looked* as if the servants of the living God were going to have a terrible defeat. We have all been in places where it seemed as though we were defeated, and the enemy rejoiced. We can imagine what a complete defeat this looked to be. They fell down into the flames, and their enemies watched them to see them burn up in that awful fire but were greatly astonished to see them walking around in the fire enjoying themselves. Nebuchadnezzar told them to "come forth out of the midst of the fire." Not even a hair was singed, nor was the smell of fire on their garments, "because there is no other god that can deliver after this sort."

This apparent defeat resulted in a marvelous victory.

Suppose that these three men had lost their faith and courage, and had complained, saying, "*Why* did not God keep us out of the furnace!" They would have been burned, and God would not have been glorified. If there is a great trial in your life today, do not own it as a *defeat,* but continue, by faith, to claim the victory through Him who is able to make you more than conqueror, and a glorious victory will soon be apparent. Let us learn that in all the hard places God brings us into, He is making opportunities for us to exercise such faith in Him as will bring about blessed results and greatly glorify His name.

Bob Brake was in charge of the petitions. He had been involved in various petition campaigns since 1964 but noted that this was the first time he had seen such a spontaneous outburst of support from the local citizenry. He shared that he had recently been in a debate with one of the homosexual leaders who admitted that he had had his first homosexual experience at age seven and didn't have any role models of adult homosexuals to pattern his life after. Brake continued that one of the purposes of this special-privileges ordinance is to provide role models for *our* growing children.

He told of a briefing session with Tony Raimondo and Steve Spooner, officers of the Coral Gables Police Department, at which they told of the arrest of a former private-school principal on homosexual-related charges. The findings opened a can of worms that stunned even the Gables investigators who had received death threats. The officers had pictures of ten- and twelve-year-old boys in homosexual relationships with older men.

Bob Brake explained: "After the petitions are back and the signatures counted, the Metro Commission will be faced with a choice. They will either have to pass our ordinance which repeals theirs, or they will have to call an election in Dade County and let the people decide. If we have a large number of signatures, I think they might very well say at that point, 'Well, this truly is the will of the people of Dade County, and there is no need for an election!' I think if we can get twenty to forty thousand signatures . . . the Metro Commission should respect that number of signatures and be favorably impressed. Then, I believe, they will say there is no need to spend upwards of a half-million dollars on an election to say we don't want to have homosexual teachers in our classrooms!"

As it developed, the people left the Save Our Children meeting that day so on fire that by the deadline one month later, well over sixty-six thousand signatures had been obtained. But as we were to see, the Metro Commission was not favorably impressed, and a costly election did become necessary.

The Bible speaks of those who depart from the truth and believe falsehood instead (*see* 2 Thessalonians 2). For five long months the homosexual activists perpetrated the big lie claiming that there were three hundred thousand homosexuals in Dade County which was carried by the local media as *fact*. I was reminded of the blowfish who is actually quite a small fish; when a larger fish looms, the blowfish blows itself up to frighten off the larger fish. The technique is employed by humans as well. It's called *terrorizing,* or putting fear into the hearts of one's enemies. This technique is being used by militant homosexuals to influence the nations' businesses, the media, the public, and politicians as well. However, in the final outcome, there was a total of a little over eighty-nine thousand votes supporting the ordinance.

We had already discovered that having the courage of our convictions was a costly matter in more ways than one! My husband, as treasurer of Save Our Children, discussed our need for financial assistance. He showed a circular distributed by the homosexual leaders that said they would need an initial thirty thousand dollars to fight us in our petition campaign. Bob said he didn't think we needed thirty thousand dollars, because we had six hundred thousand dollars' worth of good people working right there, right then. But we did need money for postage stamps, printing, and other expenses that would arise. We also discovered we needed all the financial help we could get. TV, radio, and newspaper advertising was costly. There came the time when our budget hadn't been met, and we were in quite desperate straits. I remember turning to Bob and saying, "Bob, God got us into this, and by faith I believe He's going to provide the money we need to fight this battle in the right way." The Lord honored our faith and answered by sending the money from God's people. For the most part, the money came in small amounts. It was a grass-roots response, mirroring the concern of the citizens of our land. In contrast, the homosexuals received mostly large amounts from "gay" bars, businesses, and from the sale of obscene anti-Anita Bryant T-shirts.

5
Metro's Gay Blunder

Newspapers called it "one of the most emotion-charged campaigns ever to confront the American voter." Reports reached us that the nation was looking on with alarm, hope, amusement, and intense curiosity. The Miami *Herald* reported:

> The campaign is over Gay Rights, and it has all the ingredients—from sex to religion to Anita Bryant bursting into the "Battle Hymn of the Republic"—for a national media spectacular.
>
> The media haven't missed their chance. The Dade campaign has invaded television's "Today," "Tomorrow," and "Tonight" shows; Anita Bryant and placard-waving gays have made the cover of *Newsweek;* small-town America and urban gay communities have become passionately concerned with what happens at the polls here.

We had not planned it that way; in fact, we had no intention of deliberately attracting nationwide attention. But the seriousness of the homosexuality issue in Miami struck an exposed national nerve. Metro's Gay Blunder, as it soon came to be called, focused attention on the subject of homosexuality like nothing else had ever quite done. In a very short time it became a national movement, with both factions as the subject of heated controversy.

Alan Courtney, who has been an outspoken favorite in Miami for many years on top-rated WINZ radio with his "Open Mind" program, labeled those who started the uproar in Dade County as "exhibitionists and obnoxious professional exploiters," and said all of this was "a sad commentary on our internal decadence."

Standing in the thick of the fight and facing a formidable task—the gathering and submission of petition signatures in order to place the issue on a referendum—were the concerned, often grim-faced moms of Miami.

The need for offices in various parts of the city soon was made known. Quickly they came into being, and volunteers worked around the clock. Someone had to answer the phones, commiserate with worried parents, lick envelopes, and get the word out. Someone had to canvass the supermarkets, shopping centers, businesses, and the streets of Miami to gather signatures. Day in and day out, the petitions flooded Dade County. Churches circulated them to their congregations and massive walk-ins were staged by people of the area who were zealous to protect their rights. It was simply hard legwork, at times under threat of physical harm from militant homosexuals. The closer we got to the election, the more people from all over joined the bandwagon. The amazing thing was that we had only three paid people working for Save Our Children—Tim Baer, campaign director; Susan Nay, office manager (who gave up a lucrative position to work at half her former salary); and Cathy Ellis, secretary. Public records show that a large part of the funds contributed by people from all over the nation and intended for use in advertising *against* the Save Our Children organization went to pay high salaries to the homosexual movement's leaders and workers. I think this was one reason we were able to do more television advertising—we had a great many volunteers helping us. Also, on election day the opposition spent nearly eight thousand dollars to pay for cabs to take their supporters to the polls.

With the help of Mike Thompson of Long Advertising Agency, and Bob Daly, a well-known retired newspaperman, we put together speeches such as one issued on February 11 regarding what we called "Petition Sabbath," the kickoff of our petition campaign.

I was determined that with God's help I would not be just an armchair general. Bob and I joined ranks with hundreds of others who were staying up nights, going out speaking, making phone calls, and doing all the things that had to be done. God had a grip on our hearts that was strong. Over and over again the words from Hosea 4:6 leaped into my mind, and I quoted it often in the frequent speeches I had to make:

My people are destroyed for lack of knowledge: because thou hast rejected knowledge, I will also reject thee, that thou shalt be no priest to me: seeing thou hast forgotten the law of thy God, I will also forget thy children.

Man, in his ungodliness and unrighteousness, seeking only self-gratification in his desperately wicked ways, deliberately turns his back on God by rejecting both His natural and special revelation. The Book of Romans spells it out in unmistakable terms. Because he chooses to reject knowledge and suppress the truth and because he refuses to acknowledge that he is morally responsible to a holy God, man falls into gross moral perversion, trampling upon the rights and welfare of others. We saw it happen in Miami.

As we continued to hear from every part of the country where the Dade ordinance had made headlines, I became very conscious that there was a network of praying Americans out there—people who had been praying for a long time for revival in this country and survival of the nation. I knew this was a revelation from God to encourage our hearts. We were not in this alone.

We felt an urgency. Of course we were time conscious because of our particular need in Miami, but God was impressing upon me daily the need to be swift to trust and to obey Him. The time is short. God is willing to bring revival to our country. He will act in response to the fervent prayers of righteous men and women, but *He does not want us to delay* as we proclaim the need for people to turn from their sin while there is still time.

We sent a letter to those who were standing with us in prayer. We thanked them and reminded them of Ephesians 6:12: "For we wrestle not against flesh and blood, but against principalities, against powers, against the rulers of the darkness of this world, against spiritual [hosts of] wickedness in high places."

The issue became a unifying force for Latin and Anglo church groups in Miami. But our mail also showed that it was unifying diverse groups across the country. We heard from blacks, Spanish-speaking people, and others of many nationalities and religious backgrounds. The legitimate minority groups protested against homosexuals waving the flag of human rights. They called homosexuality by its right name—a perverted, unnatural, and ungodly lifestyle.

There is a saying which is used by entertainers but has also become a rather commonplace remark: The show must go on. Regardless of personal problems and circumstances that are not conducive to performing at one's best, the show goes on. In the midst of all the pressures brought on us by Metro's Gay Blunder and our participation in Save Our Children, there were commitments to be kept and shows that had to be performed.

Those were frenzied days—a blur of shows, TV programs, constant interviews, radio programs, and meetings with representatives of the media wherever we were. I was quoted and misquoted, supported and ridiculed.

The Saint Petersburg *Times* religion editor quoted me correctly. I had told her that it would be a sin for me if I didn't speak out. I suggested she look up my favorite Bible verse—Philippians 4:13. She did and quoted it in her lengthy editorial:

> For I can do everything God asks me to with the help of Christ who gives me the strength and power.
>
>   LB

6
Mourning for America

The hurt in my heart and the agony in my soul were of such intensity that when I was home and first got the news of a national homosexual bill similar to the one in Dade County, all I could do was cry. This bill, HR2998, would have the effect of making it mandatory nationwide to hire known practicing homosexuals in public schools and in other areas. With all the other thousands of letters I received from groups all over the country dealing with pornography, abortion, TV violence, ERA, and various other things, all I could do was weep for America. There are no words in the English language strong enough to describe the grief I felt.

Bob saw that I was engulfed in a private kind of grief that even he could not console. It was a particular woman's pain that he was unable to share with me. Something rebelled deep, deep within me that even I could not explain. "God, I can't take any more of this. You're just going to have to take this off my shoulders. It's too heavy . . . I can't bear this . . . ." And, of course, that's what God wants from us—brokenness before Him. "Casting all your care upon him; for he careth for you" (1 Peter 5:7). I had really given it to the Lord, and I knew He had taken the burden. Much work remained to be done, but the Burden-bearer was going before me.

George F. Gilder has written an important book entitled *Sexual Suicide* in which he examines a wealth of anthropological, economic, social, and psychological data. He then proceeds to explain why family breakdown is the chief cause of the problems that have come down with such force upon our country in recent years. The women's-liberation programs—many of them fostered by women with lesbian tendencies—have weakened family ties and worsened these problems, he says. Gilder points to statistics that prove single men are the chief source of crime and social disruption. He argues convincingly that marriage is essential to male socialization in the modern world. Gilder eloquently states:

> Women control not [only] the economy of the marketplace but the economy of eros: the life force in our society and our lives. What happens in the inner realm of women finally shapes what happens on our social surfaces, determining the level of happiness, energy, creativity, and solidarity in the nation.

The "inner realm" of my being was sickened and repulsed by the "sexual suicide" path the "gay" movement was advocating. Gilder says it so well:

> In the end, the sexuality of both men and women—and the spirit of the community—is reduced to the limited, barren, compulsive circuitry of uncivilized males. Confined in a shallow present, with little hope for the future or interest in the past, neither sex works or loves devotedly. While sex is given a steadily larger role, it loses contact with its procreative sources and becomes increasingly promiscuous and undifferentiated, homosexual, and pornographic. It becomes what in fact our current liberationists—male and female—already imagine it to be. It becomes in essence a form of sensuous massage . . . .
>
> Thus sex is losing its very character as sexuality. No longer governed by the normative syntax of procreative love—no longer responsive to the differing sexual configurations of mature men and women—erotic activity becomes a shapeless, dissolute, and destructive pursuit of ever more elusive pleasures by ever more drastic techniques. In the quest for a better orgasm or more intense titillation, a frustrated population goes on ever wilder goose chases in "little-known erogenous zones"—on ever more futile scavenger hunts for sexual

exotica, picking up a whip here, an orgy there—but always returning to the increasingly barren and shapeless lump of their own sexuality. Such are the aporias of carnal knowledge—the dead ends of "spontaneity."

He describes homosexuality as a "flight from identity and love," the "gay liberation" movement as an "escape from sexual responsibility and its display a threat to millions of young men who have precarious masculine identities." Women's liberation he looks upon as a destructive fantasy. "There are no human beings; there are just men and women, and when they deny their divergent sexuality, they reject the deepest sources of identity and love. They commit sexual suicide."

The more I read, the more sick at heart I became and the fighting spirit within me grew. I had to look up words and terms—this was a whole new area of thinking for me. "Oh, dear Lord, has this been going on all around me? I've been so indifferent, so careless . . . ."

Because I knew my Bible I recognized the perils of homosexuality. But even if one did not know or accept the Word of God, common sense indicates that homosexuality is against nature and not normal and therefore not to be encouraged.

Gilder's analysis saddened me considerably. Despite the romantic propaganda about male homosexual relationships, it is, in fact, agonizing for most of its practitioners. Lasting relationships are few and sour. Gratifications are brief and squalid—"gay" bars, street cruises, forlorn personal advertisements. These do not afford the kind of love the homosexual needs. Gilder warns that heterosexual society should not praise or affirm the homosexual alternatives or acquiesce to their propaganda. It is tragic if the cultural surroundings provide more easily for homosexuality than for recovery of normal patterns. Cities like Miami, which would give in to homosexual demands, are doing the homosexuals no favor. It is far better to help an individual recover from his dejection—whatever has led him into such a debased way of life—restore his confidence, and help him return to full heterosexuality. A society that condones homosexual behavior is a society that is uncaring, for it is allowing an individ-

56 The Anita Bryant Story

ual to fall prey to sexual self-destruction.

"Our local Metro Commissioners made two mistakes," Bob Brake said when talking to the black leaders in Miami about the homosexual issue. "Their first mistake was failing to take into account that their ordinance could be repealed through petition and referendum vote; their second mistake was that they didn't count on Anita Bryant and Brother Bill."

When Brother Bill Chapman repeated this to me he added, "No, Anita, *you* were their *first* mistake!"

7
Two Mistakes

"Why me?" I asked Brother Bill. "I mean, I'm just a woman. I shouldn't be this involved. And it's not in the Bible!"

"Yes, it is," he countered. "Anytime, throughout the Bible, when God's men didn't take their stand and were not there when God wanted them, He raised up a woman. Look at Esther; look at Deborah."

"Deborah?" I questioned. "Esther I know about, but I don't remember Deborah."

"Look it up, Anita," he kindly admonished me. "You'll find it in the Book of Judges. Life was unbearable for the people of Israel many times because they sinned against the Lord. At one such period in their history they were conquered by King Jabin whose commander in chief was Sisera. He had a mighty army with nine hundred chariots.

"The Bible says that Israel's leader at that time, the one who was responsible for bringing the people back to God, was Deborah, a prophetess." (*See* Judges 4:4.)

I listened intently as Brother Bill told me the account. Many times in the heat of the battle for Miami I recalled the story. But that day I cried out, "Is this really happening? Dear Lord, where are the religious leaders of our land who should have taken a stand on this thing long before it got this far?" I agonized over this. Deborah was the weaker vessel; yet she had the stronger faith.

God seemed to quiet my groanings in moments such as that when my own faith wasn't that strong: *Anita, you're going to ruffle lots of edges. My people are often so noncommittal, so neutral. That's the problem in America.*

I wonder how Deborah felt . . . and Esther. It was hard to separate the wife and mother in me from the outspoken woman I knew I
had to be at this crisis time in our nation. It would have been so much
easier to step out of the picture, to draw back and say: "Look, my
future as an entertainer is at stake; my family is being dragged into
something—and they deserve so much better; I've done my part,
now let the men run with the ball and let me be just me."

When I read the account of Deborah, I found myself in awe. *Dear
Lord, she was a singer!* The psalm of praise she composed became a
pattern of praise for me.

As Christians we have been quick to define our roles and criticize
women who step out of what *we feel* are their proper roles. God has
been dealing with me about this and, I believe, has been showing me
things and asking me to share them through this book and in the
stand I have taken.

If, in God's name, we would call others to their duty, then we
should be willing to assist them. God needs both the Baraks and the
Deborahs if the enemy in our land, and I mean sin in its *many* forms,
is to be routed.

The newspaper-clipping services informed us that President Carter
was number one in national clippings and what was happening in
Miami was number two. This went on for months. When we heard
this, I told my husband and others, "You know, it's as if they are
talking about somebody else. I get up in the morning, pick up the
paper or a magazine, and think, *This can't be happening to us; it's
just unreal!*"

We felt consumed by the implications of the responsibility that had
been thrust upon us. One Sunday morning at church I went forward
following the pastor's sermon and asked for more help, at the same
time praising the women who had been working so hard. But I felt
burdened and, without realizing what I was saying, I blurted out,
"Where are the real Christians who are willing to stand in this hour?"
I saw four women rise from their seats and come forward. Then I
broke down, and looking up at Brother Bill, I asked through the sobs,
"But where are the men?"

As I stood there crying, I felt so foolish, so embarrassed! Judi

Wilson's husband, Rudy, stood up and shared how he had gone out the day before and collected six hundred signatures on the petitions. Suddenly, from all over the church, the men started coming forward. One after another they said things like, "Anita, I'm sorry it took me so long to realize the need," or, "Anita, seeing you cry has made me realize I've been neglecting my duty."

The women who had been extending themselves to the point of near collapse joined me in praising and thanking God. We knew we could go no farther unless the men were not only in union with us, but were leading us.

Not only was there very little normalcy in our home those days, but it was the same in other homes where the women had been carrying the load of this burden. But after that morning, it was as if our church had stepped over an invisible line. Although the men had always been committed, now they were sacrificially committing themselves to do whatever was necessary to save our children. It was a solidifying factor, and, to our amazement, we discovered this was happening in many churches all over Dade County. It was a major turning point, as together we confronted Metro's Gay Blunder.

It was time to respond to the press. Once again we issued a press release:

> I have compassion for the families of homosexuals who have chosen this way of life. It's a choice, not a birth-right . . . . But my duty to the way of God and the preservation of my children has a higher claim . . . .
>
> What these people really want hidden behind obscure lawyers' phrases is the legal right to propose to our children that there is an alternate way of life—that being a homosexual or a lesbian is not really wrong . . . .
>
> Behind the high-sounding appeal against discrimination in jobs and housing they are really asking to be blessed in their abnormal life-style by the office of the president of the United States . . . .

8
Hello, "Gays"—Good-bye, Anita

At the outset of the petition drive in Miami, I received a telegram from the producer of Teletactics, representing the Singer Sewing Machine Company, informing me that an upcoming television series with them was being canceled. That prompted us to issue this statement to the press:

> Just twenty-five years ago, many artists and writers in the entertainment industry were blacklisted, prevented from practicing their skills, and denied their livelihoods. In response to this blacklisting, civil libertarians and liberal commentators throughout America raised their voices in protest.
>
> Today, we have come full circle. I have just been notified that the blacklisting of Anita Bryant has begun. I have been blacklisted for exercising the right of a mother to defend her children, and all children, against their being recruited by homosexuals.
>
> Because I dared to speak out for straight and normal America, because I dared to challenge the immoral influences of homosexual recruiters and their protectors on the Metro Commission . . . I have had my career threatened. I have had my First Amendment freedom of speech abridged.
>
> This telegram tells the story. It destroys the dream that I have had since I was a child, a dream to have a television series of my own, to entertain and present wholesome subjects to my fellow Americans—the kind of wholesome entertainment Bob Hope, his group, and I provided for lonesome

American veterans in the jungles and throughout the world for seven straight Christmases away from my family.

This television series, for which I was recently put under contract, has just been canceled—not because Anita Bryant lacked the talent to make the series a success, but because Anita Bryant spoke out on an immoral ordinance that would degrade our community.

Of course I am concerned about the economic penalty my family and I must pay because of the blacklisting of Anita Bryant. But what primarily concerns me is that others in our community and our nation may now be afraid to speak out against what is illegal, immoral, and corrosive to our way of life.

What also concerns me is that by caving in to the small number of vocal homosexual activists, those who sponsor American television and other forms of entertainment will give the impression that this sick segment of society represents society on a much broader basis than it does in reality.

I repeat my belief: Homosexuals do not suffer discrimination when they keep their perversions in the privacy of their homes. They can hold any job, transact any business, join any organization—so long as they do not flaunt their homosexuality and try to establish role models for the impressionable young people—our children.

I will continue to fight the attempts of Metro, and the attempts of a few congressmen who on February 2 presented a similar type bill in the Congress of the United States to legitimize homosexuality.

Homosexuals cannot reproduce—so they must recruit. And to freshen their ranks, they must recruit the youth of America.

I shall continue my fight against that recruitment. Those who do not share my conviction may continue to blacklist my talent—but with God's help, they can never blacken my name.

Over and over again we were asked, "But how did you feel? How did you react?"

I knew I was not smart enough or informed enough to deal with the total ramifications of the militant homosexual problem throughout this country. My confidence, therefore, was never in myself. But we are made of human stuff, and we did have our ups and downs, our moments of emotional upheaval and grave concern. There was so much at stake—perhaps our lives, and much of our livelihood. But still our confidence rested in God. I am certain now that God was preparing us for that telegram all along. Something deep inside me knew this was going to happen, and when it did, I was prepared for it. That's how the Lord works.

Bob received the telegram backstage while I was taping "The 700 Club"; so he was aware of the content before I was and he tried hard to protect me. In his own way he was searching frantically for a way to soften the blow. I was stunned, of course, and I remember saying to him, "Bob, I was raised with the Singer Sewing Machine . . . . Grandma Berry made all my clothes on her old treadle Singer . . . ."

I think I was so inwardly prepared, however, that nothing could have touched me at that point in my life. But I was greatly concerned for my husband, for Bob suffered far more than I did. "Bob," I said, "whatever God takes away, He puts something better in its place. Let's just praise the Lord."

The editor of the Parkersburg, West Virginia *News* is not necessarily an Anita Bryant fan, as he plainly stated in the opening paragraphs of his editorial. Nevertheless I was encouraged by his objective honesty.

> Ms. Bryant's views will be opposed by some and applauded by many more. She envisions the danger in which children are placed when a person with unnatural sexual habits holds a position of authority. She is exercising her constitutional rights, which unfortunately at this time has cost her a handsome commercial contract. That she would not cease

and desist in her campaign, nor resign her membership in an organization, "Save Our Children, Inc." is to her eternal credit . . . .

. . . She seeks only a clean and healthy relationship between teacher and pupil. But someone along the line felt she was guilty of infringement, an unproved transgression, and a violation of the laws of our free-wheeling society . . . .

We are not soliciting unneeded help for Ms. Bryant or the organization in which she so zealously operates. During these days when too many have acquiesced to standards that society a number of years ago would have regarded with extreme repugnance and utter detestation, we must loudly applaud her efforts at the expense of being cast aside by a television sponsor.

I really smiled when the Tulsa, Oklahoma, *Tribune* described me as a square gal out of Tulsa, originally, who believes in such "blueberry and apple pie things as God, country and the difference between men and women."

The Tulsa *World* fired off a round of hard-hitting observations:

The only way you can lose your job because of your personal political or social beliefs is to let it get around that you hold to the traditional Judeo-Christian view of sex and marriage.

So it has finally come to this:

A person who wishes to publicly promote homosexuality is by law protected against "discrimination" in Dade County, Fla., and some other places. But a person who opposes this special consideration of homosexuality and exercises her political rights against it is fired without recourse.

The incident confirms the growing influence of homosexuals in the TV-entertainment business. In itself, this need not be of any great concern to the public, or even any of the public's business. (Sex, whether homo or hetero, should be a private matter.)

Unfortunately, however, the militant homos seem determined not only to work in TV, but to use that powerful medium to sell and promote their sexual outlook—to make it appear "normal" and acceptable. When that happens, people whose religious and moral beliefs are offended by homosexuality have every reason and every right to protest.

The Hudson, Iowa, *Herald* came on strong with a brief statement:

> . . . It's ironic that the civil libertarians who have loudly advocated equal rights for homosexuals have failed to stand up for Anita Bryant's rights to express her opinions. What a sad commentary on our times when the rights of the majority are violated by the minority.

In all fairness to a tremendous number of newspapers, I must point out that many called into question with great frequency the fact that those who defend freedom of speech when the topic is pornography, antiwar activities, or "homosexual rights," remained silent when I exercised my freedom of speech.

The Bartow, Florida, *Polk County Democrat* questioned: "Is decency a sin?" and added:

> Miss Bryant's logic is unassailable, and her campaign extremely laudable. If fighting for decency, and for protection of children from deviate influences, is grounds for canceling business contracts, our national morals are in sad shape, indeed.

9
Backlash

I opened the mail one day after we became involved in Save Our Children, Inc., and there before my eyes was the most hideous thing I had ever seen—a picture of two nude men committing an act of homosexuality. The letter that accompanied it was filth—just filth.

I have had to cast it out of my mind many times since then, when it comes to haunt me. I do this by claiming the power and the blood of the Lord Jesus Christ. I have thought so often, *Oh, God, what must pornography do to children who have no knowledge of how to cast these kinds of pictures out of their minds and who do not know You.* I am sure such pictures must stimulate some children to the point where they are molested in their minds. The thought is enough to make any concerned parent agonize.

The people who open the mail at our offices have since come upon many such letters. But you could ask everyone who has had this experience, and they would tell you that you do not soon forget the initial shock of seeing something so perverted.

If there was any litany I spouted with frequency, it was what I told Phil Donahue on his show in Chicago. "The hardest thing to do is to convince people I don't hate homosexuals. I pray for them. We would like to help homosexuals. God says in the Bible we are to hate sin, but love the sinner."

Donahue's audience is comprised largely of housewives, and his programs turn often to the topic of feminism. One of his most frequent guests is Gloria Steinem in addition to Betty Friedan and Germaine Greer—women whose names are linked with the feminist movement. Recently he received a national Emmy award for "best host of a daytime variety or talk show" nudging out such celebrities as Dinah Shore, Merv Griffin, and Mike Douglas. The point is, he has a following and is listened to.

We shared with Donahue and his audience the views of three religious leaders in the Miami area: Rabbi Weberman and Archbishop Carroll said they would go to jail rather than hire a known homosexual to teach in their schools. Our pastor, Reverend William Chapman, said he would rather burn down the school than allow a known homosexual to be a role model for our children. He did not want them taught something that God says is an abomination and that we as a nation will be judged for accordingly. "These are very strong feelings these men are expressing, Phil," I said. "This is not a personal judgment, or just the way we happen to feel, but we believe in the Word of God."

If we were, as a country, to sanction known homosexual teachers, then to be consistent (and not "discriminate," using the homosexual community's terminology), we would have to allow idol worshipers, people living blatantly adulterous and immoral lives, thieves, drunkards, and other undesirables to enter our classrooms and pose as respectable role models. The man who has a drinking problem could carry his bottle with him into the classroom, set it on his desk, sip from it while teaching, and instruct the children that there's nothing wrong with imbibing. That is a farfetched exaggeration, Anita, you say. Oh, no, it isn't, not if you believe the Bible and 1 Corinthians 6:9, 10 which puts homosexuals in the same class as the drunkard and others mentioned above.

It was Phil Donahue's stated opinion that "the gay community has been crucified over the years." He also told UPI, "A gay can't change any more than a heterosexual can change, and that's largely misunderstood."

"Well, you wouldn't know it in Dade County," I answered in response to his charge that they've been "crucified." "In Dade County they have 'gay' bars, 'gay' hotels, 'gay' baths, and many 'gay' publications." There are homosexual magazines found in all large American cities.

I explained that the Coral Gables Police Department has a sheet their undercover men have found. If a homosexual comes to Dade

County, Florida, and wants to know where the young boys are, the sheet tells him. "Phil," I said, "I would have to disagree with you—homosexuals are not discriminated against in Dade County."

A family who attends our church school owns a rental-car agency. While cleaning out one of their rental cars, they found a book *The 1977 International Gay Travel Directory* and turned it over to our pastor. The book spells out explicitly anywhere you want to go, right down to the bathrooms and stalls at university campuses and businesses, where the homosexual can find what he is looking for. There is a coded key in the front of the book clueing the reader in on the kind of individual or crowd and what kind of acts he can expect. (After finding out that this information exists, it is no wonder that the militant homosexuals are interested in insuring against discrimination in "public accommodations.")

I reminded the listeners and the visible TV audience that the Bible speaks this way of sin and sinners:

> Know ye not that the unrighteous shall not inherit the kingdom of God? Be not deceived: neither fornicators, nor idolaters, nor adulterers, nor effeminate, nor abusers of themselves with mankind; Nor thieves, nor covetous, nor drunkards, nor revilers, nor extortioners, shall inherit the kingdom of God. And such were some of you: but ye are washed, but ye are sanctified, but ye are justified in the name of the Lord Jesus, and by the Spirit of our God.
>
> 1 Corinthians 6:9–11

This tells us that although a person may be a homosexual (or be guilty of any of the other mentioned sins), he can make a deliberate choice and come out of it. "And such *were* some of you," the apostle Paul said to the Corinthian Christians to whom this letter was addressed. Plainly that is past tense. "There is an answer today for the homosexual, for any sinner," I emphasized, "and that is to be willing to repent of his sin, not to flaunt it or to be proud of it, but turn away from it. Nothing could be more plain."

One of the callers said she considered herself to be a Christian.

She had taught Sunday school, was a high-school teacher, but she was a homosexual. I explained to her that we cannot take out of the context only what we want from the Bible. We have to accept the whole Bible, and its teachings on the matter of homosexuality (and other sins) are clear. We cannot separate God's love from His wrath. Jesus said, "If ye love me, keep my commandments" (John 14:15).

In the Book of Colossians the apostle Paul speaks of the new life in Christ, saying we are to mortify [put to death] such things as "inordinate affection" [sexual sins], and this includes acts of homosexuality. "For it is on account of these things [sin] that the wrath of God will come, and in them you also once walked, when you were living in them" (Colossians 3:6, 7 NAS).

Phil Donahue broke in, "Now stop it. It will be your interpretation against hers, and we will be here all day. I have read the Bible, and it is a five-hundred-year-old translation . . . . You can't believe what you read in the newspapers today, so how can you believe something written that long ago?"

Bob said, "We disagree one hundred percent with you, Phil. We believe the Word of God is as relevant today as it was yesterday, and it is going to continue to be."

Another caller voiced her support of our stand. "My son goes to a university where they have a 'gay' dance twice a year," she related. "More than a thousand boys go there and dance together. If you think that isn't a sickening thought. It's wrong . . . ."

Phil Donahue questioned: "Homosexuals want to know, Anita, what would you do if you discovered that one of your children was one?"

"I would tell him God loves him," I answered, "but that God has a standard, a judgment He must exercise. I would continue to tell my child that I love him; I would not disown him, but I would not back down in my stand that he needs to repent of that sin and that choice he has made and turn to God before he can know real and lasting happiness."

It was at this time, when we were on "The Phil Donahue Show," that we received word from the Singer Company that cancellation of the show *"had not been cleared with top management.* Singer policy fully supports her right to take a personal position on legitimate issues independent of her commercial involvement with the company.'' As it stands at this writing, an executive of Singer has visited with us, and the situation has yet to be resolved.

Although some sections of the media were kind, not all were gracious in their remarks and reporting. There were distortions of facts and comments. Statements were taken out of context. We were made to look ridiculous through coldhearted and cruel comments. Many remarks were sensationalized and blown out of proportion.

For example: *Newsweek* magazine, in a feature story, stated that I owned a white, monogrammed Rolls Royce. In fact, we do not and never have owned a Rolls Royce. I still don't understand what that would have to do with the issue.

The *Gay Crusader,* published on the West Coast, fired off a blast declaring, ''Nationwide gay backlash grows.''

> Anita Bryant is the real and burning issue which homosexuals face in America today . . . that is the considered opinion of several gay activists from San Fransisco, Los Angeles, and Sacramento. For the first time in history, homosexuals in America find themselves faced with a unified front, more or less, with ''Mrs. Clean'' Anita Bryant leading the way. Never before has the anti-gay element in America been able to rally around the firebrands who have denounced and damned into hell the homosexual.

They described my approach as being ''very smooth, and very humane,'' and that I came on ''like a loving mother.'' This they considered to be very ''dangerous.'' Bob and I were depicted as making a pleasant pitch, ''not any hell-fire damnation trip.''

> Her approach is one which is frightening, for she appears most reasonable, appearing to make sense, and using the word love often, saying that she doesn't hate homosexuals, she doesn't want them harmed. She is the most dangerous person we have ever confronted in the history of the gay liberation movement.

A Los Angeles "gay" activist said I was the most serious threat to the "gay liberation" movement in his time along with a growing number of "exgays" who had ended their homosexuality by coming to Christ. This homosexual activist said this was, to him, "frightening" and our approach "charmingly deceptive!"

A West Coast homosexual publication reported that Pennsylvania, Arkansas, and New Hampshire were making legislative attempts to repeal their "gay rights" laws which had passed earlier. And it named other states—Indiana, Colorado, Ohio, California, Iowa, and West Virginia—and groups which were organizing with an eye to placing on the ballot "antigay" legislation. The writer's reaction to that was, "It is obvious that Anita Bryant is having an effect upon the American people."

The GLA (Gay Liberation Alliance) coordinated demonstrations against the sale of Florida citrus products in various places and boasted of it in this same publication. They coordinated another one at the Singer Sewing Machine Center in San Francisco under the banner "Help Sew Up Anita's Big Mouth."

Bob and I and others who were involved in the Dade County battle were much in prayer, always concerned with the ramifications involved and the hurt that might come to others by what was said or done. We expended much energy in our concern over this. We knew what it meant to come under great stress. It was a battle—no doubt about it—and we were caught in the cross fire of verbal shots taken at us personally. But we were fighting the issue. Never once did we attack people, politicians, the five Metro Commissioners, or those who opposed us. The opposition, however, resorted to other tactics. This is still going on as you read this.

Newsweek magazine as late as June 20, 1977 was saying that our advertisements were "exaggerated denunciations of homosexuals as 'human garbage.' " They reported Ethan Geto, one of the campaign advisers for the homosexuals, as stating, "The campaign was fought with an enormous amount of confusion and distortions and lies. But the community down here bought the big-lie technique . . . ."

In contrast, our opinion is that the campaign was very informative and clear on exactly what the issues were. We feel the public was fully prepared to cast an intelligent vote—regardless of which way they voted. Had we lost, we would have felt that we had done our best and that the people just did not agree with our position.

The militant homosexual activists brought in Jim Foster from the staff of San Francisco Mayor George Moscone, and Ethan Geto, on leave from the staff of New York City's Bronx Borough President Robert Abrams. Money poured into Miami to aid them in their fight.

One interviewer from the Oak Park, Illinois, *North Suburban* wrote her reaction to interviewing and asking me tough questions: "You feel like a sunshine tree has fallen on you." I told her:

> If people are discriminated against now under the civil rights law they can take it to court . . . Homosexuals are not a race. It is not a birthright to be a homosexual. A lot of them are under the misconception they've been a homosexual all their lives . . . . A homosexual is not born, they are made.
>
> If they [homosexuals] are a legitimate minority group then so are nail-biters, fat people, short people, whatever. The laws of the land have always been to protect the normal, not the abnormal. It you're going to have a preferential legislative piece for everyone in the whole world, it becomes ridiculous . . . .

It not only becomes ridiculous, it puts the law of the land on the side of the unrighteous!

Another writer describing the rallies related that some were pro, some con. "Hysteria flamed to fury. Men began to accuse each other. It was dangerous to wear cologne. The attorney general of Florida got into the act by declaring, somewhat gratuitously, that homosexual acts are against the law . . . ."

I can truthfully report that wherever we went, we did not see people who supported us in hysteria but rather, the shouting and the mania were on the part of the militant homosexuals. In one instance, in Kansas City, where we attended the annual Christian Booksellers Association convention, one of the booksellers was spat upon by a picketing, foulmouthed "gay" activist.

The *Guardian* in London, England, assessed the referendum and the Dade County situation and reported that the United States Weather Bureau had announced the first hurricane of the season would be called Anita.

> Last week Hurricane Anita struck Miami—in the person of a former Miss Oklahoma who managed to combine the symbols of motherhood, religion, and patriotism in a sweeping victory over the rights of homosexuals. Anita Bryant, more than anybody else, was responsible for the unexpected large margin by which voters in Miami have just become the first major constituency in the nation to reject an attempt to give homosexuals equal rights.
>
> At 37 Ms. Bryant is more than a glamorous and younger version of Britain's Mary Whitehouse . . . . Does her victory mark the beginning of the end of the permissiveness of the last decade? It would be premature to believe so.

He reported accurately that the surprising thing about the gradual surfacing of homosexuals in American life in the last few years was a classic case of liberal reform by stealth. Up until Miami there had never been a referendum on the issue in any city. Local legislatures had been able to pass so-called antidiscrimination ordinances and regulations without the glare of publicity.

The current state of affairs shows that Congress has shown no inclination to pass a bill introduced by Representative Edward Koch (NY) and his thirty-eight cosponsors which would amend the 1964 Civil Rights Act to "outlaw discrimination on the basis of affectional or sexual preference." The bill is bottled up in various subcommittees, and at the state level, no legislature has yet passed a bill preventing discrimination against homosexuals in public. And thirty-two states still restrict sexual acts in private between consenting adults.

Jonathan Steele in Washington for the *Guardian* asked questions which others throughout the nation are increasingly asking:

> . . . after Miami will politicians now react with even greater caution? Will any cities beyond the 40 which, like Miami,

already have ordinances preventing discrimination against homosexuals in housing, jobs, and public facilities, now reverse them? Will other cities hesitate before introducing them? Equally important, the confidence of homosexuals themselves could be sapped, so that the trend for them to come out into the open will stop. In other words, will Hurricane Anita soon blow itself out, or is this a time for putting up the shutters for another long season of storms?

What the general reading public does not know, however, is that the names for the hurricane season in Florida were "selected nearly ten years ago," according to the U.S. Department of Commerce, National Oceanic and Atmospheric Administration National Weather Service. The press has, of course, capitalized on the opening of the hurricane season to ridicule my character much to the embarrassment of the director, Neil L. Frank, and others at the National Hurricane Center who have apologized. If "Hurricane Anita" in actuality were to be a devastating killer, one can imagine how the media will use that, and, if it fizzles out, I'll get called on for that as well. In a situation such as ours, one is at the mercy of those who mold public opinion.

THE EDITOR — Opposing

Bryant

In the middle of so much mail...a subject.

ALEXIS ELIOTT

Let's set the record straight...

12-A   THE MIAMI HERALD   Monday, April 4, 1977

Officials of Save Our Children,
Gay Activists Debate Ordinance

FROM PAGE 1A

'Metro's ordinance prohibits parents from sending their children to private schools which do not employ homosexuals because schools cannot, by the ordinance, deny them employment.'

— Robert Brake

'In order for homosexuals to appear on the most remote Polynesian islands, in every age of history, without any initiation from any other culture, it must be a natural thing for a certain percentage of people to be homosexual ...'

— Robert Basker

SECTION B
The Miami Herald
Saturday, February 19, 1977

Local News

Moms March Against Gay Law

Gay-Rights Law Is Crushed

Margin of Victory
Greater Than 2-1

AN EDITOR'S COMMENTS
Anita vs. Gays: Who's Discriminated Against?

THE MIAMI NEWS   42 Pages
Miami, Florida, Tuesday afternoon, March 15, 1977

Each Side Claims 'Nature's Way'

The Gay Issue: Whose Rights Pre

Locked in debate, four men shout, seethe and stub out cigarette angrily.

TODAY'S
Q&A

ountywide vote on gay rights

The Miami Herald

Showers

Wednesday, June 8, 1977   Florida's Complete Newspaper   78 Pages   Final Edition   15 Cents

Outcome an Expression
Of Fears and Emotions

ryant Rehired by TV Show Sponsor

By SAM JACOBS

Gay Leaders: We Shall Not Be Afraid
... Leonard Matlovich, Arlie Scott, C. Michael McKay

Citing Metro's "special privileges" ordinance as an "open door to homosexual recruitment," Anita introduces Save Our Children, Inc., and designates "Petition Sabbath" when Dade County citizens were asked to sign petitions demanding its repeal. (Wide World Photos) *Below:* A group called Christians Behind Anita Bryant demonstrates its support for her stand for morality outside the New Orleans auditorium where she performed. (Wide World Photos)

Anita's moving performance of "Battle Hymn of the Republic" is met with ringing applause during the Downtown Miami Kiwanis Club sponsored debate. (Miami *Herald*) *Below:* "Gays" in San Francisco Gay Freedom Day march chanting, "Human rights now." (Wide World Photos)

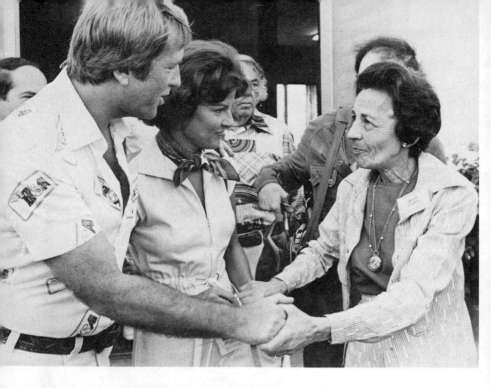

An election official greets Anita and Bob as they arrive at their polling place near their home, Villa Verde, in Miami Beach. (Wide World Photos) *Left:* Anita signs her ballot as 45 percent of those registered turned out to vote. (Wide World Photos)

A vote is cast for repeal of the ordinance which gave sanction to homosexuality—called an "abomination" in the Bible. (Wide World Photos) *Below:* Election day included last-minute handshaking. Thousands of supporters formed a worldwide prayer chain to ask God for victory at the polls and strength for campaign workers. (Wide World Photos)

"While continuing to speak out and work against those laws that sanction homosexuality, we shall continue to seek help and change for homosexuals themselves, whose sad values belie the word *gay* which they pathetically use to cover their unhappy lives." (Wide World Photos) *Below:* The results in, rewarding hours given in personal campaigning and the cost of canceled contracts, Anita and Bob enjoy the victory of doing God's work. (Wide World Photos)

The Green family's first priority after the hectic campaign is to spend
time with each other. (Wide World Photos)

"Tonight the laws of God and the cultural values of man have been vindicated," Anita declares at the press conference given after 70 percent of the voters demanded repeal of the "special privileges" ordinance. (Miami *Herald*) *Below:* "Victory in Jesus," Anita claims in song while accompanied by Brother Bill Chapman during the post-election celebration attended by more than thirteen hundred supporters at the Northwest Baptist Church. (Miami *Herald*)

10
Uproar

We were given less than thirty days to gather petitions. In that period, well over sixty-six thousand were received and the commission was faced with a decision. It either had to repeal its original ordinance or put it to a vote and let the voters decide. It chose the latter route against the advice of well-informed counsel, thus forcing upon local citizenry a four-hundred-thousand-dollar election.

The issue became one not only of morals, religion, and so-called civil and human rights, but also one of economics. Miami *News* reporter Jack Roberts reported that the "gay" Coalition announced it would try to raise the four hundred thousand dollars nationally. His explanation of this was that it was a deliberate ruse to put the "gays" in a good psychological position—the idea being to make it look as though we were costing the people four hundred thousand dollars until the "gays" came to the rescue. Roberts stated: "Gays are entitled to equal protection of the law but that doesn't mean you make them more equal than others."

Now the uproar began in earnest, and newspapers carried headlines such as: GAY REFERENDUM CAMPAIGN HEATS UP.

My husband stated: "We're working hard to win this. Otherwise Dade County will become like San Francisco where many 'gays' dominate daily life."

A Dade homosexual leader said, "This isn't just any referendum. The ramifications are enormous . . . . We're going door to door . . . we're going to plaster the city."

Both my husband and Bob Brake announced at the outset that I planned to maintain "a low profile." I have a family and other responsibilities that consume much of my energy and time. In all honesty, I had no intention of going around stumping, debating, or appearing on national television talk shows. Contrary to newspaper reports, there was no "gleam in my eye as I went national." I did intend to keep all prior bookings and to pursue my career in the entertainment industry. Mike Thompson, our adman, said to reporters, "Anita is a singer, not a debater."

The Miami *Herald* stated that out-of-staters had taken over the "gay" communities campaign and that an influx of "gay" celebrities was expected to help woo voters in what they were entitling "Operation Come on Down."

When poet Rod McKuen came to Miami, it was widely reported that he threatened to make me a national laughingstock and said, "I intend to call upon every comedian friend I know to have so many jokes go forth about her throughout the land that she will be a laughingstock such as this country has never seen before."

Contributions were coming in for both sides from the rest of the nation, but we made it clear to the press that our contributions from out of state were unsolicited. We were thankful, however, and heartened because we realized the extent to which the "gay" forces were going in their advertising—in both the print media and on radio and TV—to influence voters and gain nationwide sympathy for their cause. To counter this we needed to launch an advertising campaign as well.

The mobilization of so-called "gay" strongholds in New York and California was especially seen and felt in the Miami battle. Among other things, the National Gay Task Force from New York put together a two-page "Who's Who List of Support for Human Rights of Gays" which looked impressive on paper and was widely circulated.

Don Slater of the Homosexual Information Center in Hollywood, one of the oldest clearinghouses for information on homosexuality, was interviewed by the *Berkeley Barb*.

> Anita Bryant will probably get killed due to her anti-gay rights efforts in Florida. And that's a direct quote. Looks like the guys who run the billion-buck gay bar biz in Florida, who aren't very limp wristed, do not appreciate her number at all . . . .

Unfortunately far too many people, women especially, think of the homosexual as just that—a limp wristed type who wouldn't hurt a fly. Those of us who were in the thick of the fight in Dade County know better. While it would be unfair (and we do try to be fair and take into consideration those homosexuals who are not militant or flaunting themselves) to stereotype all homosexuals as being militant, still the more realistic picture of those homosexuals who are stirring up trouble in this country comes across as being exactly that—militant and deviate in nature, involved in sadistic sexual rituals, and abominable practices. A look at their books, their photographs in magazines, and their writings gives ample evidence that this is so.

The undisputed leading figure in the Coalition for Human Rights in Miami is John W. Campbell, described by the media as "a well-to-do operator of a chain of 40 'gay' baths," and "the acknowledged leader of Miami's 'gay' activists and a driving force in the current holy war over the rights of homosexuals . . . ."

"Unless we lose badly [in the June 7 election]," he said, "Anita could well be the best thing that has ever happened to gays. She's mobilized us all over the country. The issue is really out in the open now. There's no turning back. It has to be faced . . ."

Newsweek reported that Campbell first became fully aware of his own homosexuality as a freshman in college, and ever since then his life has been almost exclusively centered on "gay" activities. He stated frankly that he doesn't have many dealings with "straight" people, except in the Democratic Party and the American Civil Liberties Union. In Miami he is recognized as a shrewd businessman whose homosexual health clubs have "private cubicles where men can have what Campbell discreetly calls 'relationships.' "

Campbell regards me and our organization with open scorn and refers to us as "loonies" and sports a button in his lapel that reads ANITA DEAR—CRAM IT. A former Baptist, he admits to understanding my outlook, and says, "A lot of people think she's doing this for publicity, but I don't doubt her sincerity or her motives for a moment.

I know how Baptists think. There's just this feeling that homosexuals are not God's chosen people." He regarded us as formidable opponents and openly stated that Miami's homosexual community had a lot at stake in the battle. "There is no doubt," he acknowledged, "that it will be a very serious setback if we lose."

Newsweek called me "the Carrie Nation of the sexual counter-revolution," and described our efforts as "somewhat bizarre but deadly serious."

> To many of the nation's 20 million homosexuals, the vote—the first of its kind in a major city is a crucial test of whether the country is willing to extend civil-rights legislation to homosexuals. "Miami is our Selma," says one gay activist.

In the same article they reported that the San Francisco school board had voted to change its family-life curriculum to reflect homosexual life-styles. This, of course, is what the rest of the nation can expect should the laws of the land be changed eventually.

Teenagers were among those who received a pamphlet put out by the Dade County homosexual community entitled *Celebrate Our Victory*. Undercover agents in Miami found it being passed out on some Miami school grounds. The pamphlet stated:

> We have gotten a gay rights bill passed in Dade County . . . BUT, there is now a major effort to take this away! You must help yourself and unite with the rest of the gay community, with the following actions:
>
> 1. Register to VOTE . . . .
> 2. Write letters of support to each commissioner . . . .
> 3. Phone in your support to these commissioners . . . .
> 4. FINANCIAL SUPPORT URGENTLY NEEDED . . . .
> 5. Reinforce our HUMANISTIC image . . . .
> 6. Write your feelings to . . . Florida Citrus Commission . . . .
> 7. Write your feelings to . . . First Federal Savings and Loan . . . .

8. Write your feelings to . . . Orange Bowl Committee . . . .
9. Re-examine your own life, and if you can, we urge you to "COME OUT."
10. Recycle this message to 5 of your friends.

The significance of this victory here in Dade County cannot be overestimated, either locally or nationally, nor can the negative effect of its repeal. A repeal would send a tidal wave of repression all across the country.

Miami's Gay Rights Ordinance is a tremendous precedent. GAYS, NATIONWIDE, ARE DEPENDING ON US . . . .

But, we put out a pamphlet, too. It was entitled "Save Our Children From Homosexuality!" and it enraged the homosexual community. We urged readers to vote for repeal of Metro's Gay Blunder and said, Here's why:

The ordinance is not needed . . . .
It endangers our children . . . .
It is a dangerous precedent . . . .
It threatens your home . . . .
It attacks free enterprise . . . .
It debases religion . . . .
It is a peril to the nation . . . .

Any of these reasons is enough.
But the overwhelming reason is that Metro's pro-homosexual ordinance is an open invitation to recruit our children! Vote FOR children's rights. Vote FOR repeal.

The inside of our pamphlet showed local and national newspaper headlines confirming our oft-stated warning that our children were in danger of homosexual recruitment.

• TEACHER ACCUSED OF SEX ACTS WITH BOY STUDENTS
• POLICE FIND SEXUALLY ABUSED CHILDREN (*Courier News,* Elgin, Illinois, November 19, 1976)

- R.I. SEX CLUB LURED JUVENILES WITH GIFTS (Associated Press, February 17, 1977)
- OC TEACHER HELD ON SEX CHARGES (The *Register,* Santa Ana, California, March 8, 1977)
- HOMOSEXUALS USED SCOUT TROOP (New Orleans)
- TEACHER FACES ABUSE RAP
- EX-TEACHERS INDICTED FOR LEWD ACTS WITH BOYS (Des Moines *Register*)
- 4 MEN ACCUSED OF ABUSING BOYS (Detroit *Free Press,* February 16, 1977)
- SENATE SHOWN MOVIE OF CHILD PORN (San Francisco *Examiner,* April 2, 1977)
- FORMER SCOUTMASTER CONVICTED OF HOMOSEXUAL ACTS WITH BOYS

The pamphlet asked the question: "Are all homosexuals 'nice'?" These are the actual stories in the nation's press. Judge for yourself. THERE IS NO "HUMAN RIGHT" TO CORRUPT OUR CHILDREN!

The pamphlet defined what the militant homosexuals want:

The following demands are from the February 1972 convention platform of A National Coalition of Gay Organizations in Chicago:

- Repeal of all laws governing the age of sexual consent.
- Federal support for sex education courses prepared and taught by gay women and men presenting homosexuality as a valid, healthy preference and life-style as a viable alternative to heterosexuality.
- Enactment of legislation so that child custody, adoption, visitation rights, foster parenting, and the like shall not be denied because of sexual orientation . . . .

Advertising Age, a trade journal for business and industry, reported that it was me versus actor Ed Asner and former attorney general Ramsey Clark in a TV battle that was to be waged prior to the June 7 referendum. They described our ads:

One spot . . . features Ms. Bryant, her husband and her children in a garden setting. She tells the audience that she and her husband have for months stood up for their family, for "your family" despite "vicious personal attacks" from the opposition. Her husband asks the people to vote and to protect the children of Dade County against the threat of homosexual influences "in our schools and play grounds."

Another Bryant spot contrasts a scene at the Orange Bowl parade with a San Francisco parade of homosexuals in which "men are hugging other men, cavorting with little boys, wearing dresses and makeup." Warning that the "same people who turned San Francisco into a hotbed of homosexuality want to do the same thing to Dade County," the voice-over asks people to vote for decency and the human rights of their children on June 7.

Almost every day saw the opposition's forces converging on Miami. Leonard Matlovich, the former air force sergeant who was discharged after disclosing his homosexuality, was quoted in the Miami *Herald* as stating: "We're running this campaign as seriously as if we were electing a president of the United States."

We have to agree with Ralph Renick, vice-president and news director of WTVJ (Channel 4), Miami, who said "Publicity in America is a powerful lord. It gives fame and can take away fortune . . . ."

For some time I had been scheduled to perform at the grand opening of a wholesale fruit market in southeast Minneapolis during the month of May. It was one of the few entertainment bookings we had, and Bob and I were determined to keep it. There, as elsewhere, we were picketed and confronted with protesters. Some of the more militant picketers wore signs designating themselves as fruit marshals. "I love the homosexual enough to tell him the truth," I stated. "I'm not out with a Bible in one hand and a sword in the other. That's not my style. I have stood in love and for the defense of my children. The truth about homosexuality is that it is a spiritual problem . . . ."

11
Power in Prayer

Very early in the battle I felt the Lord was telling me to start a weekly prayer group in our home. I argued with Him. *Lord, I've got all this pressure, all these meetings, these people coming and going, the family . . . . How can I start a prayer group?*

The answer I heard was unmistakable: *Trust and obey. You need to come before Me and pray more than ever before.*

If my people, which are called by my name, shall humble themselves, and pray, and seek my face, and turn from their wicked ways; then will I hear from heaven, and will forgive their sin, and will heal their land.

2 Chronicles 7:14

I have been questioned about my frequent use of such expressions as "the Lord told me," "waiting for God to direct us," and "listening to the Lord." In Houston I explained to reporters that I have never heard God speaking in the sort of supernatural, audible voice that such phrases imply, but that many times God puts thoughts in my mind. The best way to know the character of God is to know His Word—the Holy Bible. I have come to know Him this way so intimately that He speaks to me in my thought patterns.

The Bible describes Christians as the Body of Christ here on earth. I have known this all of my adult Christian life, but I had never experienced it quite as I did when women from all walks of life and from all denominations met every Thursday morning at my home for an hour and a half to pray and seek God's guidance for personal and national problems and to praise Him for the many answered prayers.

When you move in obedience to what you feel God is telling you to do, be prepared for Him to respond. I cannot describe to you the love I felt from these women and how encouraged we were by those precious hours spent together.

The Bible teaches that we *have* not, because we *ask* not. We claimed the dominion and power of Christ, and we expected Him to move on our behalf. Some of the results of our prayers were immediately evident. God brought me to the point at which I could not be intimidated by the opposition. As the weeks passed into months, and even with the overburdening demands on me, I became stronger instead of weaker because of prayer. And, in fact, I was strongest at the end of the campaign.

I especially felt the power of prayer when we appeared on the nationwide television programs. David Hartman was very cordial, but he asked some loaded questions on the ABC-TV "Good Morning, America" program, and as viewers saw, when I started replying by quoting the Bible, we were cut off the air nationwide—"accidentally," they said.

It seems Gore Vidal had been deliberately set up to follow me on this program and he claimed he had never heard such expounding of hatred since the Hitler regime. "She's either full of hatred or stupidity, or maybe a little of both and it is time individuals recognize this." Incidentally, he was not "accidentally" cut off.

Experiences like that were exhausting, and there were many of them. Following that program we went back to the Warwick Hotel in New York City where, upon arriving the night before, we had realized we hadn't been there since our wedding night. It brought back beautiful memories, and Bob and I needed that. God blesses us in unexpected ways.

I felt God's presence and power and knew after the experience on the "Good Morning, America" show that I could answer anybody and anything. The Lord had prepared me.

The "Who's Who" CBS-TV crew came to the house and filmed an interview. Dan Rather was to have interviewed me, but he came down with the flu; so Barbara Howar came instead. Barbara was nice but tough with her questions, but I felt ready and didn't waver in giving answers. We invited the crew's wives to join us all for dinner. While we finished up the remainder of the shooting, the wives pitched in and prepared a beautiful dinner. These were very meaningful occasions, and the coverage on the telecast was fair to both sides.

It was a whole new world for this woman! Always before my life had been so structured and private; now suddenly new friends were ringing my doorbell, I was hostessing teas for up to four hundred women, and impromptu meetings might happen at any time of the day and night. At all times there was an incredible atmosphere of unselfish love and giving.

Another loving and thoughtful occasion was a surprise birthday-party luncheon given for me by some close friends from my church. They presented me with a crewel embroidery work that reads: MEN MUST BE GOVERNED BY GOD OR RULED BY TYRANTS (William Penn). Food, fellowship, and fun in the midst of chaotic days—it meant a lot.

The Florida Conservative Union hosted a dinner under Mike Thompson's leadership. Representatives came from all over the state and from other states as well. It was a tremendous gathering that brought together some of Florida's outstanding conservative leaders and individuals, both democrat and republican, who believe that by banding together they can better inform themselves of activities important to the state and country at both the congressional and at the state-legislature levels. Their support was of great value to us. They had invited Ronald Reagan also as special guest, and Mike Thompson introduced him by saying, "Anita, we flew in a fruit picker from California. Would you come up here so we can make a presentation?"

Ronald presented me with some California oranges and said, "Because of the orange freeze here in Florida, we figured you could use these." Of course it brought down the house.

"Really now, how can you do this to me?" I replied.

"It's really to show appreciation, Anita," he answered.

"But you know I can't eat them," I countered.

"I understand," he laughed, "but don't eat them, just squeeze 'em!"

There was laughter again, and it was what we all needed. Later they sang "Happy Birthday" to me and presented me with an award. I sang "Battle Hymn of the Republic" back to them to show my appreciation. I was deeply touched. "Freedom's never been free; it's always been bought with a very high price," I said. "It's not America that needs changing, it's people. And only Almighty God and faith in Him can get right down to where the heart of the problem lies . . . ."

Later that week Florida's Governor Reubin Askew came out in opposition to the ordinance when asked a question about the homosexual issue during a press conference. He said he would refuse to hire a homosexual as a member of his staff. "I've never viewed the homosexual life-style as something that approaches a constitutional right, so if I were in Miami, I would have no difficulty in voting to repeal the ordinance," the governor said.

We heard from senators and state representatives from almost every state in the country. Typical of their comments are these: Senator Marion Menning, who led the successful fight in Minnesota against the state's "special privileges" law, stated, "It's a threat to my personal rights; it's a threat to my religious beliefs." State Representative Tom Collier of Arkansas, who introduced a resolution in the Arkansas House commending us in our fight, commented, "When God's law and the country's laws conflict, God's law should be supreme." The Oklahoma Senate, which passed a resolution submitted by Senator Mary Helm, praised us for "patriotic and high minded performances . . . ."

We heard from many who took offense at the "gay" community and their choice of the word *gay*. Many columnists devoted whole columns deploring the fact that the homosexuals have taken a perfectly good word and twisted and perverted it. Was there ever a more tragic misnomer? As the title of his article "There Is Nothing Gay About Homosexuality" indicates, Murray Norris points to statistics which show that 50 percent of all suicides and homicides in big cities can be attributed to homosexuality (according to Judge John M. Murtagh in his book *Cast the First Stone*).

Another cause for these astonishing figures is that the homosexual very often is an extremely lonely person. Norris writes:

One of the biggest problems with homosexuals is their own loneliness. In homosexuals' own publications, in the writings of psychiatrists who treat them, in the words of the ministers who try to help them, there is this constant repetition of the loneliness of the homosexual life. This loneliness has led many homosexuals into drugs and alcoholism . . . .

Dr. Melvin Anchell, medical doctor and practicing psychiatrist, points out that homosexuals are seldom satisfied with their relationships and are constantly seeking new thrills, or new forms of sexuality. They head into sadomasochism. They are frequently vicious with their own partners and with others.

Whoever decided to call homosexuals "gay," must have had a terrible sense of humor . . . .

Norris cites the publication *VD* which says half of the cases of syphilis in this country can be traced to homosexuals. Doctors say the rampant venereal disease among homosexuals is due to their constant search for new partners and the lack of protection.

Reading things like that makes me long to reach out and help the homosexual. At the Reverend Charles Couey's South Dade Baptist Church in Homestead I said: "I am so grateful . . . even when our bodies have been stretched out to the very end of our strength, even when our minds have gone about as far as they can go as to what to think of to say next, when our emotions have been drained to the bottom of the barrel . . . that is when the Lord really takes over." I am finally beginning to realize what my favorite Scripture is all about: "I can do all things through Christ which strengtheneth me" (Philippians 4:13).

I thank God that in the sea of life, when the storm comes up so fast and the waves get higher than your head, and they look like they are going to consume you, that way out yonder there is a Lighthouse—Jesus.

12
The Militant Homosexual

"One thing Anita Bryant has done is make concerned people aware that they have to get off their duffs and do something political . . . ." The speaker was not an Anita Bryant fan, but rather Massachusetts Democrat Elaine Noble who was described in the San Francisco *Examiner* as having the historical distinction of being America's first legislator to admit publicly being homosexual.

This lesbian state legislator is an outspoken advocate of "gay rights." Speaking engagements take her from one end of the country to the other as she espouses "gay" doctrine and urges homosexuals to run for political offices on city and state levels. She says it would be more effective for homosexuals to get states to pass antidiscrimination laws than to rely on U.S. Supreme Court test cases. "Homosexuals need laws that will give them the equal right to sue somebody," she states.

It is shocking to realize how many legislators have capitulated to the demands of the outspoken defenders of homosexuals. Perhaps the most disturbing thing of all is the suddenness with which the "gay" liberationists have surfaced as a full-fledged social-protest movement.

An Associated Press report datelined WASHINGTON is a good example:

> The Federal Communications Commission was petitioned to require radio and television stations to pay more attention to the problems, needs and interests of homosexuals.
>
> Jean O'Leary, co-director of the National Gay Task Force, told a news conference, "We are asking FCC to add leaders

of the gay community to the checklist that broadcast licensees must use in their community-ascertainment surveys . . . ."

Carol Jennings, who wrote the petition, said it seeks an end to the twofold problem of "invisibility of the gay community in radio and television programming or stereotypical treatment of gay people in the broadcast media."

Who would have thought a few years ago that anyone would pay attention, much less give newspaper space and television coverage, to a man shouting, "I'm gay, I'm proud. There is nothing I am prouder of. I am infinitely proud of the accomplishments of gay people. And I am going to shout it from the church tops, from the highest mountain, for always, and forever."

That same homosexual declared, "The most vociferous national enemy we now face is Anita Bryant . . . if we do not organize against them [the Save Our Children campaigners], we will deserve whatever they have in store for us . . . . Stand up and be counted," he urged as he passed out literature asserting, "Anita Bryant eats lemons."

As far back as August, 1971, *Newsweek* did a six-page report on the growing "gay liberation" movement. As I read it now, I am startled and, at the same time, sickened by the realization that it took me so long to wake up to what is happening. And I cannot help but wonder how many others there are who feel the same way. Could we have prevented this? Have we been derelict in our duty both as citizens and Christians? Must other communities be confronted with it on a local level before they wake up? And then will it be too late? How will the young mother who attacked me so viciously feel when her child falls victim to the advances of a homosexual?

That *Newsweek* article reported their many ways of assertion, as "Out of the closets and into the streets" became their rallying cry. Attorney Ellis Rubin of Miami Beach said, "They are asking us to carve out a new civil right based on their sexual appetite."

Praise is in order for legislators like U.S. Senator Jesse Helms (R, N.C.) who are watchdogging what is happening in Washington, faithfully reporting their findings, and calling upon the American people who believe in decency and morality to stand up and let their voices be heard.

A report which Senator Helms sent out to his constituency was widely circulated and brought tremendous response our way. We reprint it here because it is representative of the kind of unsolicited support we received.

WASHINGTON—During the past few weeks, I have talked by telephone on numerous occasions with a fine, Christian lady whose face and voice are familiar to most Americans. Her name is Anita Bryant. She has stood beside Billy Graham during his televised crusades. No doubt you have seen her also as she appeared on television commercials advertising Florida orange juice.

She is a lovely person, deeply committed to Christianity. She is also a concerned American—concerned about the erosion of moral principles in her country. She has spoken out against pornography and indecency in all of the forms spreading across America. She has warned that unless America returns to basic principles, our freedoms are in jeopardy.

Not so long ago, she spoke out against America's growing tendency to give respectability to homosexuality. And that's when her troubles began.

LEGISLATION—In particular, she condemned legislation introduced in the U.S. House of Representatives on January 4 by Congressman Edward I. Koch (pronounced "Kosh"), a member of the New York delegation in Congress. Mr. Koch was nominated by both the Democratic Party and the Liberal Party of New York. The bill that he introduced bears the number H.R. 2998.

The title of Mr. Koch's bill states that its purpose is to prohibit discrimination on the basis of affectional or sexual preference . . . .

Specifically, the bill would amend the so-called Civil Rights

Act of 1964 in several ways. Among other things, employers would be required by federal law to seek out and hire homosexuals on a quota basis. This would include schools, hospitals and other institutions. Failure to comply with the requirement (to hire homosexuals) would result in the loss of federal aid.

TROUBLE—When Anita Bryant dared to speak out against this bill she found herself in deep trouble. In Miami, her home city, the homosexuals (who call themselves "gays") organized, and began a pressure campaign to intimidate the Singer Sewing Machine Company, which was to have been the sponsor of a television series featuring Anita Bryant.

Anita's contract for the television series was abruptly canceled. An official of the Singer Company made clear that, all of a sudden, Anita Bryant was "controversial."

Controversial? Here was a fine and decent lady, a dedicated Christian, who had dared to speak out. And because she did, her contract was canceled. Small wonder that business people in America today are so rapidly losing the respect of the citizens of this country. If this is an example of the courage of those who are the greatest beneficiaries of the free enterprise system, it is a clear indication that if and when the free enterprise system dies, it will be suicide, not murder.

PROUD—I am proud of Anita Bryant. In my several conversations with her in recent weeks, I have pledged my full support to her.

I don't know whether the Koch bill will be approved by the House of Representatives. But this much I do know: If and when it gets to the U.S. Senate, I will fight it with every means at my command, with every bit of strength I can muster.

Maybe you'd like to drop Miss Anita Bryant a note of encouragement. If so, send it to me, and I'll make certain she receives it. She is fighting for decency and morality in America—and that makes her, in my book, an All-American lady.

The California Citizens for Decency have put together a disturbing report. They state:

As the number of homosexuals in strategic positions increases, so does their appetite for power. In an interview with L.A. *Times* critic, Cecil Smith, TV producer James Komack stated: "Do you know the most powerful lobby in the entertainment business? Bigger than blacks or women's lib or any nationalist or racial group? It's the gays. If you don't have the approval of the Gay Media Task Force, you don't go on the air."

. . . As the organizing and lobbying goes on across the country, the National Gay Alliance has made it abundantly clear that their Number One priority . . . is passage of the National Gay Rights Bill in Congress.

While senators like Jesse Helms and organizations and individuals from all over were standing with us, one of the homosexual leaders, codirector of the Miami Victory Campaign, told a news conference at Metropolitan Community Church in New York, "Anita Bryant is a very, very dangerous person . . . ."

And in California a Christian bookstore reported receiving bomb threats. They also discovered that someone had inserted between the pages of various books a circular crying out: "Save Us From The Anita Nightmare."

A "Gay and Christian" conference at Kirkridge Retreat Center in Bangor, Pennsylvania, adopted a resolution deploring my "misuse" of Scripture to "attack gays" and my "willingness to deny civil rights to them."

The board of elders of the Universal Fellowship of Metropolitan Community Churches charged that my campaign was "both un-Christian and un-American." They adopted a resolution urging that "attempts be made to educate Ms. Bryant and her supporters through debate and confrontation."

And a top official of the National Council of Churches charged that my "antihomosexuality campaign misrepresented certain Christian positions and stereotyped homosexuals."

Troy Perry, founder of Metropolitan Community Church, writes:

> In America we are changing political attitudes. Candidates for public office now actively seek our help and our endorsement. We have begun voter registration drives in the gay community (300,000 in Los Angeles). We lobby in local units of government, in state legislatures and in Washington. We picket, we march, we demonstrate. We are beginning to feel our political muscle, and to show it where it counts.

The so-called "gay rights" dialogue in Dade County forced the subject out of the closet for churches and church leaders as well who were confronted with the issue. *The Episcopalian* magazine observed: "Now it is a common, if prickly, agenda item for vestry and deanery meetings and diocesan conventions."

As of this writing, denominations including the United Presbyterian Church, the United Church of Christ, the Presbyterian Church in the U.S., and the American Lutheran Church have studies underway as to the position they will take. Reluctantly they are being drawn into the "gay rights" debate. Some ministers within these denominations, however, regret the position papers and statements which are under study. "It does not treat homosexuality as a sin," a Nashville, Tennessee, minister said, reflecting the views of large numbers of pastors. "It makes fuzzy the issues that the Bible makes clear. The Scripture presents homosexuality as a sin."

Evangelistic Social Action magazine reported that the ambivalence of many denominations is "the classic liberal cop-out . . . the church's current official stance is ambiguous nonsense . . . . It is not civil rights that are at stake, but something much more central to the Christian witness . . . ."

The Bible has something to say about those churches who will not stand true to the revealed truth of the Word of God:

> I know thy works, that thou art neither cold nor hot: I would thou wert cold or hot. So then because thou art lukewarm, and neither cold nor hot, I will spue thee out of my mouth.
>
> Revelation 3:15, 16

The only way this terrible tide can be turned is if parents—like you, Bob and I—who feel that the fabric of society is being torn to shreds, will rise up and defend the moral principles we believe in.

13
There Is Hope for the Homosexual

I have many letters, cassette tapes, magazine articles, and books, all of which have one thing in common—these are the testimonies of former lesbians and homosexuals who made contact with us to share that *there is hope and liberation for the homosexual.*

A liberated lesbian stated that for twenty-eight years she had been a militant, bona fide radical, lesbian feminist. One night Pat Robertson on "The 700 Club" telecast pointed out the Bible passages where God condemns homosexuality, and said, "There is deliverance for homosexuals . . ." She cried out to Christ for that deliverance.

> I had cheered in the gay lib parades, and shouted happily for every advance in our gay movement . . . .
> I did not know how or if I could stop the life-style, the filthy language, the dirty thoughts, the wicked desires, the pills, the bad friends, the TM and the rest, but I gave it all to Jesus . . . and I was literally transformed—mind, soul, spirit and body . . . .

Those who minister to homosexuals say it is a bondage almost unequaled in the spiritual world. Both history and Scripture give clues as to the seriousness and depth of this bondage and the consequences. God has ordained sexual identities innate in male and female; so homosexuality is a twisting of divine order. History has shown that a national acceptance of homosexuality is often the point at which divine judgment falls upon a civilization (*see* Jude verse 7). We can point to the account of Sodom and Gomorrah (*see* Genesis

18, 19); the perversion of the nations which inhabited Canaan when Israel was ordered to drive them out completely (*see* Leviticus 18:1–24; Numbers 33:51–53).

World history and the records of Rome, Greece, Egypt, and other once-great civilizations also fell under divine judgment.

As I see theologians and scripturally uninformed church men and women trying to explain away the clear teachings of the Word of God, I cry out with my pastor, who said, "I love the homosexual enough not to allow him to assert for himself a life-style the Bible teaches is a perversion and will destroy him. I love him enough to take a stand and say, 'No, that ought not to be!'"

While we were in Sun Valley, Idaho, following the Dade County vote, the Boise *Idaho Statesman* reported the broad divergence that exists in organized religion and among theologians these days when it comes to dealing with the biblical aspects of the debate on homosexuality. Kevin LaHart reported that revisionist interpretations by modern biblical scholars are redefining the Genesis story of Lot and the mob of Sodomites to mean a serious breach of hospitality (on Lot's part). You will be hearing more about that as homosexuals themselves take up that refrain.

Modern psychology and medicine as well as some theologians, purporting to have the answers as a result of studies, have opened their arms in acceptance of homosexuality and state, as Father John J. McNeill did on "The Phil Donahue Show," "There is only one law in Christianity and every other law spells that out, and that is, 'Love your neighbor as yourself.' Any use of Christianity as a way of discrimination, of generating hatred, of putting other people down, and of making out of them second-class citizens, is definitely in conflict with the basic spirit of Christianity." We disagree since we believe one can embrace the sinner, but the Bible teaches that we should not open our arms in acceptance of their sin.

Author Roy Hession, in his marvelous little book *Forgotten Factors,* devotes one chapter to the subject of homosexuality. He reminds the reader that the Almighty does not take an indulgent view of the matter and points out that crime is the transgressing of the laws of the state; sin is the transgressing of the laws of God. The forgotten factor is that God utterly condemns homosexual practices. Even though the law of the land may say that homosexual practices are no longer criminal, *they are still sin.*

The first thing the homosexual caught in this problem must do if he wants God's help is to agree with Him and call it sin. This counsel might seem to be lacking in compassion and sympathy, and at variance with what some modern psychiatry would tell a man. But the Bible way is so often at variance with modern thought and when we encourage a man to call such a thing sin it is not to torture him with a deepened sense of guilt, but rather to assist him to take the first step toward deliverance. For if homosexuality is not sin, but simply an unfortunate trait in his make-up, he is stuck with it for life; there is nothing much that can be done about it, except to learn to live with it. Indeed, a psychiatrist said to me, "We do not profess to cure a homosexual, but only to turn a miserable homosexual into a happy one." Perish the thought! But if a man is willing to call it sin, then there is *every* hope in the world for him; there is a Saviour whose blood cleanses from sin; and he will find that the acknowledgment of sin is a man's best qualification to meet the Savior. He will find that Christ's redemption is custom-made for such a man as he is and His power is available to free him from everything he is willing to call sin.

Newsweek magazine asked the question: Are homosexuals sick? For years the view by many in the field of psychology and medicine was that it was a "disorder," and that "society doesn't produce homosexuality . . . . a traumatic childhood does." The official diagnostic manual of the American Psychiatric Association explained for years that it was "a sexual deviation" ranked with sadism, masochism, and fetishism. But in recent years, a growing number of psychiatrists have come to share the "gay liberation" view that homosexuality *per se* is not an illness but an alternate life-style. Finally the APA made history by removing homosexuality from its list of mental disorders and issuing a statement in support of homosexual rights. It did not, however, represent the majority vote.

As one does research, he discovers that even the majority of medical scientists are not in total agreement. Much of what has been written is unproven and prejudicial. The Miami *Herald* medical writer did an article and entitled it "Origins of Homosexuality Elude Scientists' Inquiry." The reason is not difficult to understand—you cannot pinpoint sin under a microscope or isolate it in some lab. Thus, the claim that one is born destined to be a homosexual cannot be substantiated. Since clinicians themselves are not of one mind regarding the homosexual problem, so it is folly to make the so-called findings of some of them the norm of our own thinking, as I have seen so many individuals (including Christians) do. This is simply taking the testimony of Scripture and making it bend to fit the world's view; this has always been incompatible with biblical truth. The permissiveness of our present culture is not our guideline; we must be guided by the Word of God. It does not endorse homosexuality or even adopt a neutral stance.

I have talked to many former homosexuals and lesbians personally. One of the most exciting moments in all of this was leading several homosexuals to Christ. Bob and I have a deep burden to continue to minister to them in whatever direction God leads us. We are learning that all Christians need to be educated and to be more sensitive in how to cope with the problems and needs of the individual homosexual.

Christianity Today, along with other Christian periodicals, Christian organizations, Christian leaders, and individuals, calls for renewed dedication:

> . . . to uphold God's high standards of purity, to feel compassion for men and women trapped by their own sins, and to go out into our society with a message of hope and salvation in Christ. Like Jesus did, we should go where sinners are and there bring God's judgment and healing grace. Homosexuals are not freaks or strange creatures in a world of straights. They are human beings, made in God's image, people to whom

God's message comes in exactly the same way it comes to all of us. Homosexuals must not be left with a stern word of condemnation from a distant and repulsed body of people called the Church; instead they must be faced with a Church, with Christians, with a God who reaches out to bless even through condemnation.

I am in agreement with Dr. Harold Lindsell who reminds us, ". . . love is not enough . . . truth is also important . . . . Good feelings cannot deliver the homosexual from the judgment of God. If he does not repent, he is doomed, but he is not alone. So are all other unrepentant sinners. God is no respecter of persons; He is also no respecter of one's sexual appetites. Hell will be partially populated by 'caring, honest, whole persons' who are proud they are gay."

14

Homosexual Teachers: Are They Dangerous Role Models?

"Most gay people as they grow up—in their church, school and home—are not aware of any gay adult, so they have no model. Most homosexuals think they are the only ones in the world, that they are absolutely isolated and, therefore, they grow up with all sorts of feelings of self-doubt and even self-hatred. It would be so important that there be some gay teachers in the schools who could serve as models for that one in ten children who is gay."

That is the statement made by Father John J. McNeill, a Jesuit priest who was introduced on "The Phil Donahue Show" as "the moral theologian, one of the founders of the New York chapter of 'Dignity,' an organization of Catholic homosexuals, and presently a student at the Institute of Religion and Health in New York." Phil brought him on the show to present "the other side of the theological viewpoint," since Father McNeill is also the author of a very controversial book, *The Church and the Homosexual.*

After Father McNeill made the statement quoted above, Phil Donahue quickly stated, "That is the sticky point, for if those teachers are going to be models, those people who are on the other side of this spectrum are going to come right back at you and say, 'We got you now because you are admitting that these people can be role models, so why are they also not going to be role models for heterosexuals who are going to admire them and then think they are wonderful and say why don't we try it?' "

Father McNeill's answer was, "We have had heterosexual role models for that one out of every ten homosexual children for centuries and it never changed them. Sexuality is given and is unchangeable, and as they grow up they become aware of what their sexuality is. If homosexuals, they need a role model of how to live out a good life as a homosexual."

My primary concern was voiced as a mother, not as an entertainer. Known homosexual schoolteachers and their possible role-model impact tore at my heart in a way I could not ignore. Two things in particular troubled me. First, public approval of admitted homosexual teachers could encourage more homosexuality by inducing pupils into looking upon it as an acceptable life-style. And second, a particularly deviant-minded teacher could sexually molest children. These were possibilities I was unwilling to risk. Added to these concerns was my deep-rooted biblical orientation which condemns the act of homosexuality. For me not to have stood up in protest would have been something my conscience could not tolerate. I had that right as a mother, a citizen, a voter, and a tax-paying resident of Dade County.

The homosexual community rhetoric made it appear that I had unfounded fears. But there are men of science who do agree with my views. Dr. Herbert Hendin, Director of Psychosocial Studies at the Center for Policy Research in New York, reminds us that society has a stake in heterosexuality and the family, as well as a responsibility to insure that homosexuals who are performing their jobs are not harassed or fired for their sexual lives. He does emphasize, however, that this does not mean that we have to approve of militant homosexuals' demands to teach children that homosexuality is an acceptable alternate life-style or to teach homosexual sex-education classes in public schools on a par with heterosexual sex-education classes. Doctor Hendin wrote this in 1975 for the New York *Times*.

Doctor Shirley Van Ferney, who counsels troubled adolescents and is a member of the psychiatric staff at New Jersey's Medical Center in Princeton, advises parents to fight the militant homosexuals' demands. She warns:

> Homosexuality should be put back in the closet where it belongs . . . the gay rights movement sweeping the U.S. is a threat to the nation's children.

Constant media coverage of the gays has made their life-style appear to be commonplace and acceptable rather than unusual and deviant . . . . This is particularly disturbing to those who are concerned that their children could easily be misled into thinking that homosexuality is an attractive kind of life-style to adopt.

Parents are absolutely correct to be fearful of the effects all of this is having on their kids . . . .

Homosexuals are so active on high-school and college campuses that there is hardly a child in America who has not been exposed to their influence.

You have a right to raise decent children in a decent society. *But that right will be taken away from you unless you make yourself heard.* If parents capitulate to the homosexual influences which surround them, society as we know it will be destroyed.

New York psychiatrist Charles Socarides says homosexuality flies in the face of the one fact we know, which is that male and female are programmed to mate with the opposite sex. This is the story of two and a half billion years of civilization, and any society that hopes to survive will have to recognize this. He further declares:

There's no doubt in my mind that if homosexuality is further normalized and raised to a level of complete social acceptability, *there will be a tremendous rise in the incidence of homosexuality.*

It would have dire effects for society.

Homosexuality militates against the family, drives the sexes in opposite directions and neglects the child's growth and sexual identity.

Doctor Samuel Silverman, associate professor of psychiatry at Harvard Medical School, urged parents to "protest vigorously if any of their children's teachers are professed homosexuals." He said what others of us have been saying all along—it's admirable to be tolerant and sensitive to people's civil rights, but what the militant homosexuals are seeking *cannot be classified as legitimate civil rights*—and "a homosexual teacher who flaunts his sexual aberrations publicly is as dangerous to children as one of the religious cultists." This psychiatrist underscores what those of us who stood in protest feel so strongly—the militant "gays" are not fighting for their own civil rights but are, in actuality, *attempting to win converts to their way of life.*

The National Observer explored the subject of whether or not homosexual teachers are dangerous role models and described California's current superintendent, Wilson Riles, as being "one of the few school administrators who will discuss the issue on the record. He acknowledges gay rights under the law, but draws the line at advocacy." Riles explains: "When you have a teacher who becomes an advocate of his or her own sexual behavior, this goes beyond why that person was hired . . . . It then becomes an exhibitionist situation. It's really not our job to try and justify any kind of sexual behavior."

Another Californian who backed our stand was U.S. Senator S. I. Hayakawa who believes it's all right for employers to refuse hiring homosexuals because of sexual preference. "Civil rights doesn't entitle a person to a job and never has. I would be very, very hesitant to allow homosexuals in the teaching profession," the seventy-year-old former educator added. He said he would have voted with us to repeal the Dade County ordinance.

In all the exchanges of words there was one thing frequently overlooked—children have rights, too. In describing the boldness of the libertines, one editor expressed the belief that it is perhaps not coincidental that as the more liberal life-styles come into the open, divorce rates soar, leaving the debris of human tragedy behind to suffer. The debris? Our children. His column reported:

A Grand Jury in Florida indicted the headmaster and a group of homosexual teachers for recruiting and sexually abusing students in a private school. This goes a long way toward proving homosexuals DO recruit and DO prefer their partners young. Thus we believe Miss Bryant's group, "Save Our Children," is aptly named.

My files are daily increasing in size as material reaches me confirming that children are being lured into homosexual activity in schools by homosexual teachers.

It was Gables Youth Resource Officer Tony Raimondo and Officer Steve Spooner along with John Sorenson who took special interest in our Miami situation and brought many such cases to our attention.

> A lot of regular people have the general attitude of "live-and-let-live" about homosexuality. People generally presume that in the homosexual world, it's a case of a couple of guys living together and not bothering anybody.
>
> That simply is not the case.
>
> A couple of guys might live together for a while, but eventually one of them is going to get tired of it and go out looking for new kicks. He will go looking for a boy; he will start occupying bus station rest rooms or whatever, or will become a Boy Scout or Cub Scout leader.
>
> We've found them in the Big Brother programs, among the staffs of youth centers, in the Foster Home program.
>
> I will say that no community, in Dade County or anywhere in the country, is unaffected.

Actually, enough material has been gathered for a complete book on the subject of child pornography and sexual exploitation of children. The Washington *Star* (April 11, 1977) reports that children have become commodities and are bought, sold and traded for the financial gain of involved adults. This newspaper states that child porn peddlers are aided in their efforts by such groups as the American Civil Liberties Union (ACLU), which believes censorship of such material violates the First Amendment protecting free speech. The horror described by a Los Angeles police officer when he saw a photo of a man about thirty and an eight-year-old boy performing

sex, was akin to what I felt upon opening the mail in our home in the
early days of the Miami battle.

> "What put me to work," said Lloyd Martin (head of a
> special six-officer unit with the L.A. Police Department that
> deals with sexual exploitation of children) "was one pic-
> ture . . . . The look on that boy's face . . . . No amount
> of words can describe it. It wasn't fear. It was more a look of
> 'somebody help me' . . . ."
>
> In order for pornography to survive, there must be a new
> product. They'll do anything to make that almighty buck.
>
> Authorities say that perhaps 70 percent of the child porn
> market now involves young boys—"chickens" in the
> vernacular—and adult male homosexuals. A vast and well-
> organized network caters to the "chicken" trade with books,
> movies and boy prostitutes . . . .
>
> Equally depressing is the ultimate effect of this activity on
> the children themselves. Those studying the problem feel the
> children will suffer lasting harmful effects and . . . will proba-
> bly grow up and become sexual abusers themselves.
>
> Said Dr. Vincent Fontana, a child sex abuse expert at New
> York's Foundling Hospital: "There is a great deal of
> psychological scarring of these kids, and God only knows
> where they will end up . . . ."

Morrie Ryskind, writing in the Los Angeles *Herald-Examiner,*
pokes fun in a sad sort of way at the local jet set for whom homosexuality is considered "in." He speaks of one such individual who
lauded a TV film on the subject as a "towering achievement of
sensitivity." Ryskind's reaction was that it was "a sleazy tale. Towering achievement, my foot. This was a wretched bore." Ryskind reported that the general manager of the TV station said he had no
qualms about showing the film at 8:00 P.M. when children could view
it, because he felt it would provide "greater understanding and acceptance of homosexuals by all ages." Ryskind continued, "Now I
can respect the quiet gays—but not the flaunters. I resent the attempt
to make it appear to impressionable youngsters that the gay life is

equal to or perhaps superior to the norm . . . ." He calls their efforts "phoney semantics," and ended his column by saying, ". . . one vote for Anita Bryant."

The Chicago *Tribune* presented a series of four exhaustive articles dealing with the subject of child pornography and ran headlines on one front page, SICKNESS FOR SALE. Among other shocking things they labeled what was happening to children as "emotional and spiritual murder."

> A nationwide homosexual ring with headquarters in Chicago has been trafficking in young boys . . . . The ring is masterminded by . . . a convicted sodomist . . . . His closest associate is a convicted murderer and thief . . . .

The report included the story of Gerald S. Richards, one of the midwest's leading child pornographers, and described him as "a flesh profiteer who fed off the young, who filmed, processed and sold child pornography film, who sold the sexual services of his young male models . . . . For all anyone knew, he was a school-teacher . . . ."

More than ten years ago the Miami *Herald* sounded a serious warning entitled "Morals Squad Takes Homo Issue to Parents" (April 12, 1966). Two detectives of the Dade County Sheriff's Department were lecturing at junior high-school assemblies and PTA meetings, warning even then of the widespread recruitment of juveniles into homosexuality. "Innocent youngsters and apathetic parents are a dangerous combination," the detectives said. "One of the major recruitment systems operates within the schools . . . ."

Miami citizens did not respond. I pray to God this will not happen elsewhere across our land and that what I have told you in this book, and in this chapter particularly, will rouse you from your apathy.

Homosexual teachers: Are they dangerous role models? What could be more convincing than what you have just been reading? I quote William A. Rusher, respected journalist, who writes:

> A teacher of young children . . . plays an important part in shaping their attitude toward many things. Without even in-

tending to do so, teachers convey to their classes, in a thousand subtle ways, their concept of what is "desirable" and what is "undesirable," what is "wise" and what is, or may be "unwise." Rightly or wrongly, many generally tolerant parents, who have no particular objection to their children being taught by homosexuals who do not reveal their sexual orientation, are concerned at having them taught by self-proclaimed homosexuals.

 . . . . today's self-proclaimed homosexuals tend to be defensively aggressive on the subject. The crux of the matter is whether, at any age when a child's ultimate sexual orientation may still be undetermined, there should be placed over it—in authority, in loco parentis, and implicitly as a model of conduct—a teacher who insists upon publicly affirming his or her own homosexuality and treating it as simply "one valid alternate life-style."

15

Who Is on the Lord's Side?

If you want the blessings of God, you need to go God's way. We read in Exodus 32:26: "Who is on the Lord's side? let him come unto me." The Bible records what happened to nations who forgot God. God doesn't change; His laws don't change. We need the blessings of God on our land. As a nation, we have stooped so low in sin that we can hardly be regarded as Christian anymore. *Christianity Today* magazine points out, "Our society is going through a period of profound cultural unrest and open moral degeneration . . . . The propaganda for a homosexual life style is part of this moral unrest."

Early in the battle for Miami, Catholic League *Newsletter* commended us for our courageous fight for the religious-freedom rights of parents, and they offered to help (which they did). We were encouraged by a letter from Barbara B. Smith, General President of the Mormon Churches Relief Society, which stated in part:

> On behalf of the one million members of the Relief Society, Women's Organization of the Church of Jesus Christ Latter-day Saints (Mormon), we commend you for your courageous and effective efforts in combatting homosexuality and laws which would legitimize this insidious lifestyle. We congratulate you on the overwhelming victory of your forces in Florida Dade County elections.
>
> We stand with you in your worthy efforts to strengthen the family and the home, the cornerstone of America's strength. The men and women across our nation, concerned about the world fibers of our country, will also join in the fight against the disruptive influences to our homes, such as pornography, homosexuality, and growing permissiveness.

The Presbyterian Journal did an interview. The final question asked was: "In other situations where Christians face other battles, what would you say to them by way of encouragement, based on what you have experienced?"

My answer was, "Just three words: Trust and obey! You don't have to have expertise and a great organization to do great things for God. Just put yourself on the line and He'll bring the expertise to you along with encouragement and even the necessary funds. You can trust Him. The key is to be obedient—whatever God says to do, do it as quickly as possible.

"I do believe that in the matter, nationally, God has given America space to repent. In any case, the greatest blessing a Christian can experience is to know you are right with God even if the whole world calls you a bigot."

On Mother's Day (May 8, 1977), I was asked to appear on Jerry Falwell's "Old Time Gospel Hour" which is telecast in many cities coast to coast. Providentially, we believe, that program was aired in the Miami area on Sunday, June 5, just prior to the referendum vote. Reverend Jerry Falwell was among the few evangelists in this country who openly rallied to our cause and has raised funds to help Save Our Children. Understandably, we are deeply grateful to him and others who unselfishly, sacrificially, and generously have and are supporting our efforts.

Certainly one of the highlights of the Dade County campaign occurred on Sunday night, May 22, at the Miami Beach Convention Center, when several of this country's finest Christian leaders—Dr. Jerry Falwell, Dr. Adrian Rogers, Dr. John Huffman, Jr., Dr. Jack Wyrtzen, and Dr. D. James Kennedy—along with Mike Kolen, linebacker for the Miami Dolphins, Calvin Rose from the Miami Shores Presbyterian Church, Lee County Sheriff Frank Wanicka, "Cops for Christ" (singing in their uniforms—very moving and impressive), and ninety other men of God from all races and religions, participated in a great "Christians for God and Decency" rally. We did not instigate this; we did not ask Dr. Falwell and Dr. Wyrtzen to come and spearhead this event. It was the largest gathering of local Christians since Billy Graham had been to Miami in the fifties. Doctor

Falwell is head of Liberty Baptist College and pastor of Thomas Road Baptist Church—our nation's largest Baptist church and Sunday-school ministry—and Dr. Wyrtzen is head of Word of Life Ministry, one of the largest nationwide youth ministries. They were conducting a rally on the East Coast when poet Rod McKuen came out with his statement about his intent to make me "a laughingstock." These men saw how McKuen was raising funds to help the homosexuals. They turned to each other and said, "Look what the homosexuals are doing, and nobody in this nation is doing a thing to help Anita and the group down there in Florida . . . ."

These men of God canceled their own engagements, and when I appeared on Jerry Falwell's show he said, "We want the biggest place in Miami . . . . God has told us we are to come down and stage a rally to help you, and we're going to do it."

We were overwhelmed! "Jerry, we can't help you with this," I protested. "Much as we want to, we can't do it. We are up to our necks . . . ."

"Anita and Bob, just reserve the Civic Auditorium for us and we'll do the rest. We don't need you to do anything except show up for the rally."

And that's exactly what we did. Jerry Falwell sent his man, Bill Faulkner, a dear man of God and a professional in public relations, to come down and do all the legwork. As we traveled to the auditorium the night of the rally, it was bumper-to-bumper traffic all the way. Bob let out a whoop of joy, "Look at the buses!" How could we miss them. Buses and automobiles streamed in from every part of Florida, jamming the freeways.

Once inside the center, Bob and I couldn't believe our eyes—wall-to-wall people. The convention center was packed. It was reported that more than ten thousand people were there—and many were turned away.

We shared the platform with our own pastor and others who had worked so untiringly with a zeal and dedication I've never seen matched anywhere for anything. As we walked in, the sound erupted and I felt very strange. They were giving us a standing ovation! Brother Eddie Evans from our church led the combined choirs from many churches with the accompaniment by Jack Connors, Gail Smith, and Pat Macauly. Joy surged over my whole being; I was beside myself with emotion. I wanted to touch and embrace all those people, God's people. It turned out to be one of the most thrilling nights of our lives.

Following that rally, a woman from Miami called the Save Our Children offices and suggested a worldwide prayer chain would be in order. The girls in the office sensed God's direction and began obtaining names and making phone calls.

This prayer chain, including a group in New York City of more than sixteen thousand people, circled the globe. From as far away as Australia, Mexico, Canada, South America, New Zealand, Rhodesia and Ghana West Africa, rallies and prayer support groups dedicated our situation to the Lord. With all these people praying and working together, we knew beyond the shadow of a doubt that victory would be ours—would be God's, that is—to His Glory.

16
Victory!

It was a sweeping victory! The message from Miami on June 7, 1977, was loud and clear. By a margin of more than two-to-one, citizens of Dade County overwhelmingly voted their revulsion toward homosexuality becoming an acceptable, normal life-style. The vote—202,319 for repeal (69.3%), and 89,562 against repeal (30.6%)—overturned the controversial ordinance that had become the focus of the homosexual rights struggle nationwide.

Voter participation set a record—45 percent of the county's registered voters turned out. As voters rallied behind our efforts for repeal, they were, in effect, agreeing that this ordinance was an affront to God's law.

With Bob and the children standing beside me, that evening I gave a statement to the press:

> Tonight the laws of God and the cultural values of man have been vindicated. I thank God for the strength He has given me, and I thank fellow citizens who joined me in what at first was a walk through the wilderness.
>
> The people of Dade County—the normal majority—have said, "Enough! Enough! Enough!" They have voted to repeal an obnoxious assault on our moral values despite our community's reputation as one of the most liberal areas in the nation.
>
> All America and all the world will hear what the people have said.

No doubt our emphasis on scriptural references citing homosexuality as a sin helped to swing votes. That, and the work of our hard-

core foot soldiers—God's people. But we also know that many tolerant, broad-minded citizens voted for repeal because they felt uneasy
at the prospect of an avowed homosexual becoming a role model for
their children.

Dispirited but defiant homosexuals and members of the opposition
gathered at Miami's Fountainbleau and Dupont Plaza hotels for what
they hoped would be a victory party.

The papers reported Jean O'Leary, executive director of the National Gay Task Force, as saying that the defeat supplied "all the
evidence anyone could need of the extent and virulence of prejudice
against lesbians and gay men in our society."

But the violence and demonstrations were not instigated by those
who rallied to our support. Cities across the nation carried the victory
news, and television cameras showed what the newspapers the next
day described as "raucous" demonstrations.

Bob Daly, our hardworking director of press relations, charac-
terized San Francisco as a cesspool of sexual perversion gone rampant. It is estimated that 100,000 of the city's 660,000 residents are
"gay." More than 5,000 militant homosexuals and their supporters
marched and chanted through downtown streets there to protest the
landslide antigay vote. "Two-four-six-eight, gay is just as good as
straight," they shouted. The demonstrators held hands, hugged, and
sang "We Shall Overcome" as they waved candles.

"Brothers and sisters lift up your lights and show Anita," one
protester hollered. "We're gonna burn her out."

There was more chanting: "No more Miamis" . . . "Fight
back!"

One bartender announced that screwdriver cocktails would be
discounted from ninety to fifty cents if customers agreed to squeeze
their own California oranges. "Take your hostility out by squeezing,"
said the bartender.

The president of the San Francisco association of local "gay" bars
said, "We'll meet Anita head-on wherever she decides to try next.
Nobody's giving up."

San Francisco's sheriff returned from Miami after participating in press conferences, speaking to private groups and rallies, and taking part in the Dade County homosexual campaign strategy sessions, and told reporters: "Anita says she's been chosen by God to lead a crusade against sin. Personally, I have always been a little suspicious of people who claim to hear the voice of God." When asked about the reports of our plans to carry our campaign to other parts of the nation and if it bothered him, he said, "I don't think the people of this country are going to take seriously anybody who talks about speaking with God." This, on the heels of our smashing victory in Dade County!

But San Francisco's large and politically active group of homosexuals let it be known that they were prepared for the next battle. From the mayor on down there were outbursts of rage with heated rhetoric. "We're not going to give up," said David Goodstein, publisher of the nation's largest "gay" newspaper, *The Advocate*. "I sort of look at it like a war metaphor. We had an army of recruits. Now, we have an army of veterans."

Newspapers estimated that nearly a thousand supporters of so-called civil rights for homosexuals marched through New York's Greenwich Village for two consecutive nights demonstrating against the Miami vote. They went from one bar to another, picking up cohorts for the demonstrations, and shouting, "Gay rights now!"

They ended up outside the home of former congressional representative Bella Abzug, at two in the morning. She told them, "It's a long fight and you're not going to win it tonight. You have to continue fighting tomorrow and the next day and now you should go home."

Chicago homosexuals and their supporters held a candlelight vigil at midnight but saved most of their demonstrating until we came there to keep a professional singing engagement on June 14. The two thousand demonstrators who picketed my performance at Medinah Temple on the Near North Side were not a friendly welcoming committee! Shriners had staged a fund-raising event in observance of Flag Day and I was scheduled for a forty-five minute concert long before the Dade County so-called "gay" rights issue surfaced.

We tried to keep the lowest possible profile in Chicago and elsewhere. We went to great lengths, in fact, not to be visible so we would not fan the flames of any unrest there. We felt responsible to the people who had invited us to come and who were not involved in this issue. We also felt for the city of Chicago, the taxpayers, and the law enforcement people. We didn't hold a press conference. As Christians, we believe what the Bible says about "turning the other cheek" when reviled, and we were determined to do that. We saw the picketers with their obscene signs, and we heard their chanting and yelling. In spite of efforts by the Chicago police, eight persons were taken into police custody. All of this happened just a little over a week after the Miami vote.

A film titled "Gay USA" has been produced by twelve camera crews plus a helicopter camera crew, documenting the Gay Pride marches in New York, Los Angeles, San Francisco, Chicago, Houston, and San Diego. All crew members were volunteers and *Variety* (August 24, 1977) described the project as a "non-profit venture . . . the brainchild of director Arthur J. Bressan, Jr., conceived on 'Orange Tuesday,' the day singer Anita Bryant won the anti-homosexual referendum in Dade County, Florida." Producer David Pasko was quoted: "Our hope is for the film to play as readily to liberal-minded straight audiences as to the gay sub-culture." He considers the film comparable to a gay "Woodstock." Pasko hopes the film might be used by localized gay groups for fund raising, and that it might be used "as well as an educational tool for young people, police academies . . . and even on network television."

Jack Campbell, leader of the Miami campaign, said, "We'll continue from here. We've unified the gay community and brought national attention to the issue."

One of the most blatantly anti-God statements to come out of the entire battle was from Arthur Bell writing in *The Village Voice* from New York. "Lying in the sun, reading the Book of Leviticus (from the Bible), I decided it's time for a new Bible featuring the preachings of Steinem, Vidal, Hamill, Salinger, Hellman, Capote, and Liz Smith. Wisdom changes with the decades. Old flames should be left to die."

He left a number of people off that list, of course, including Midge

Costanza, head of the White House liaison office who enthusiastically endorsed the Dade County ordinance and accused me of having "visions of grandeur."

Human Events magazine pointed out the risks the Carter Administration is running in playing up to the counterculture set. Among other things, they were alluding to the three-hour meeting with homosexuals on March 26, at the White House which Ms. Costanza arranged. "What the Carter people will do now in pushing the counterculture is unclear, but it's hard to believe that they will want to—*a la Midge* Costanza—tangle again so early with the heroine of Miami," reported this Washington-based magazine.

President Carter himself refused to take a stand on the issue of "gay" teachers although he has stated that he does not consider homosexuality "as a normal sexual relationship. I don't feel that it's a normal interrelationship . . . ."

Like President Carter, I stand for human rights, but unlike Ms. Costanza, I do not favor the granting of special privileges which violate the constitutional rights of normal Americans. Before the next election, millions of fellow born-again Christians will demand to know if our president is in favor of a known practicing homosexual's teaching in public, private, and religious schools. The members of my prayer group and I continue to pray for President and Mrs. Carter and their family and all government leaders in hopes that they will take a stand for this issue of morality.

I don't think I can say anything more powerful about our victory than the statement by William Safire quoted in the Miami *News* about the "gay's" defeat:

> Militant leaders of the gay rights "movement" cannot minimize the defeat they suffered at the polls in Miami this week . . . .

17

Aftermath

In the aftermath of the victory at Miami, we were confronted once again by the press. This time they wanted to know our plans for the future.

I had let it be known that the national debate provoked by the Dade County referendum had united and strengthened us as a national movement, and that with God's help we would prevail in our fight to help repeal similar laws throughout the nation which attempt to legitimize a life-style considered by many to be both perverse and dangerous.

Our statements were misconstrued to mean that we intended to treat the Miami landslide as a license to launch a vast national crusade. Bob and I emphasized, as did Bob Brake (cofounder of Save Our Children), that we had no plans to go on a nationwide witch hunt against homosexuals. We said we would help by education or by sending a representative to help oppose local "gay rights" laws "only when invited by a group of substantial citizens in a community."

David Rothenberg, writing in *The Village Voice* questioned "The Future of an Illusion" *prior* to the Miami referendum. "I take issue with gay men who are under the illusion that this shadowed sex represents liberation," he stated. He made some discerning observations about the future of the "gay" movement, such as, "The Anita Bryant crusade may create a few giggles among the gay cognoscenti of New York City and San Francisco, but I have little doubt that if she gets her issue as an election day referendum, it will be Ms. Bryant who will win."

Jack Campbell boasted in Miami that even though they had gotten

131

beaten badly, the war was just beginning, "We're coming out of Miami with national unity and momentum."

Time magazine revealed that at week's end (following the vote), twenty-eight menbers of the board of directors of the National Gay Task Force, representing a number of homosexual organizations throughout the country, met in New York City to plot a nationwide strategy. It was said that activists in San Francisco, Chicago, New York, New Orleans, Houston and San Antonio were ready to picket me wherever I turned up.

There was continuing reaction—pro and con—in the weeks immediately following the Miami referendum. I was called "the lightning rod" for the "gay rights" fight which gives little indication of slowing down.

Upwards of 350 "gay rights" supporters hooted with derision and 125 of them noisily left a meeting where they had gained entrance in Norfolk, Virginia, the day after our Miami victory. We took part in a religious crusade on behalf of the New Creation Center (a counseling center and retreat). Wire services called it "The God versus Gay Confrontation." If was the first of many that followed in rapid succession, as I fulfilled a few bookings which had been on my itinerary for months.

At the Norfolk meeting, at the first mention of the word *homosexuals* the demonstrators yelled a loud no and got up and marched out. They carried signs that read THAT'S THE WAY GOD MEANT US TO BE and SAVE OUR COUNTRY FROM ANITA BRYANT.

Just prior to their outburst, I drew applause from the homosexual delegation when I said that, apart from the grace of Almighty God, I am a sinner like everyone else.

Then I began reading from First Corinthians, chapter 6, verses 9 through 11, about the unrighteous who will not inherit the Kingdom of God. It was when I read the part about sexual perverts that the commotion began. Bob and the children rushed to my side, fearing I might be harmed. There was booing, but is was drowned out as a standing ovation swept the arena.

It was an emotional time for me. I couldn't control my crying. I wanted the homosexuals to hear the last part of those verses I had been reading: ". . . but ye are washed, ye are sanctified, but ye are justified in the name of the Lord Jesus and by the Spirit of our God." My prayer that night, and today, is that the homosexual will hear these words and claim these promises of cleansing by committing his life to the Lord Jesus Christ.

As we have traveled around the country since last June, we have been met with demonstrations and pickets. At times, as in Houston, New Orleans, and Chicago, we have been warned not to have the children accompany us on account of the threats being made. It has been difficult for all of us and, according to the media, plans have been made for picketing to accompany us wherever we go. Under these circumstances, Bob and I have been reminded of what the Scriptures say regarding what we are going through: ". . . When the enemy shall come in like a flood, the Spirit of the LORD shall lift up a standard against him" (Isaiah 59:19).

At the annual Christian Booksellers Convention in Kansas City, booksellers and publishers witnessed what newspapers described as "Some 400 persons, many from the homosexual community, demonstrate in protest of an appearance." I sang at an evening concert sponsored by the Christian Audio-Visual Corporation, and then crossed the street to the music hall to appear on a telecast being taped by "The 700 Club" with my publishers.

Booksellers were warm and friendly, tremendously supportive and kind. I was able to tell them and the press that whatever I have suffered has caused me to identify more closely with Jesus' sufferings.

One of the most uplifting showings of support came from the 3500 teenage girls polled nationwide who voted me America's Greatest American—an award presented at the Miss Teenage America Pageant. Throughout that week, this pageant also was marred by militant homosexuals' picketing.

A few weeks later, the much-needed and long-anticipated vacation with our family in Sun Valley was interrupted, following our return from the services at the Central Baptist Church in Hailey, by sixteen placard-carrying demonstrators who chanted, "Anita go home—leave Idaho alone."

The demonstrators attracted the attention of diners seated outside the inn, tennis players on the courts, and other residents living along the condominium-lined street where we were staying. It infuriated us, and it took some doing to comfort and reassure the children.

Idaho Representative George Hansen (R, Idaho) publicly apologized in the *Idaho Statesman:* "To descend on Miss Bryant and her family, who only came to Idaho as private citizens to enjoy a vacation, is a gross violation of their privacy and is totally inexcusable . . . . Anita has not caused any loss of privacy or real rights to gays and their confederates which they had not already forfeited by an irrational clamor to force acceptance of their private lives on the public," he said. The Sun Valley management assured us such incidents wouldn't happen again; so we continued our relaxing vacation.

There were good things that happened, too. The Southern Baptists at their yearly convention adopted a strong resolution written by Dr. Robert S. Magee and presented by Rev. Don Wainwright which commended me for the "courageous stand against the evils inherent in homosexuality." They spoke out against the "radical scheme" of "gays" to "secure legal, social, and religious acceptance by portraying homosexuality as normal behavior, [when it is] sin."

Other Christian groups—churches, organizations and individuals—sent telegrams, resolutions, letters, and page after page of signatures from concerned individuals, letting us know we were in their prayers, congratulating us on the Miami victory, and assuring us of their continuing support.

In a vote of confidence, the Florida Citrus Commission decided to retain me as its advertising spokesperson. Ed Taylor, executive director of the State Department of Citrus, read a statement released to UPI which supported me and said, "The staff sees no need to change from our established marketing program at this time." His recommendation was based on two separate consumer research studies that showed 89 percent of those interviewed were not affected negatively in their feelings toward me, in the department's advertising, or in their intent to buy orange juice.

As we sought escape from the pressure and the press with our children at Sun Valley, I came upon these words in my favorite daily devotional book: "There shall be a performance . . ." (Luke 1:45). It explains what we are seeking as far as the Lord's guidance is concerned with regard to the future. I do not intend to be the "matriarch of a new movement," as one newsman put it. But I do intend to stand by my convictions. I do not intend to abdicate my right to be heard or to surrender our way of life and our children's future to the perverts, the smut peddlers, and the morally bankrupt.

Homosexuality is just one area that the organization may be involved in. Because of a legal suit brought by the Save the Children Federation, we have changed the name to National Committee to Protect America's Children, but we will not change what we stand for. Right now, from indications we have received, the organization has already made its impact in several cities where they were trying to push through similar kinds of legislation. We have gone national for the purpose of educating and helping those communities that seek help and want to stand on their own. But God is going to come through with answers to our prayers as to the precise direction He wants us to take and how He wants us to go about it.

Everybody has been wondering where we will go next with the organization. Mike Thompson, our communications director during the referendum, responded to that question in the August issue of *Conservative Digest.* He emphasized that we're not going to go riding into towns on white horses. If called in, we may provide seed money to get local organizations started, and we'll give the benefit of our experience so others can save time on basic research.

Mike explained: "We had many traditional Democratic groups. Catholics generally vote Democratic here [Dade County], but they went overwhelmingly for repeal of the ordinance. The Jewish community generally votes from 90 to 95 percent Democratic and they supported us. The blacks, who generally vote 90 to 95 percent Democratic, came out for repeal. And the working section in South Dade, which generally votes Democratic, went 85 percent for repeal.

"Religious leaders of all denominations were heavily involved, since, unlike public schools, religious schools were not exempt from the ordinance. Protestants, Catholics and Jews—all coalesced. For example, of the thirty-one Dade County rabbis who took a position, twenty-seven supported us . . . ."

Tim Baer, our campaign coordinator, sent a warm note to the staff, workers, and volunteers of Save Our Children in which he stated: "When I first came here, I was the 'politico.' Now, I hope that you see that politics is not a dirty word. It is a process of bringing like-minded people together for a common goal and with a common motivation.

"In this case, our goal was clear: repeal the ordinance. But, this campaign had an unusual motion. Different from all the other campaigns I have ever worked on. That motivation was the real spirit of a living God that lives within each of you. Many earthly ideals, principles, and political theories have caused men to achieve great things. But I see more clearly now what man can do when empowered by faith . . . ."

I am not a preacher, not a well-known religious figure as is Billy Graham. But I have become an enigma to the militant homosexual community. Readers should be aware that new efforts will be made in the future to neutralize me in the minds of the people of this nation. The "gay" activists have stated that they will seek to limit my effectiveness just to the religious arena.

There will be an increasing number of attacks on the religious community to make us all look pathetically uninformed, narrow-minded, bigoted and to show our efforts as ridiculously futile. Militant homosexuals will seek to play the tune and expect the media to dance.

During Gay Pride Week, at a rally in Boston, the speakers stood under a banner proclaiming CHRISTIANITY IS OUR ENEMY. As part of the program, a "gay" leader read from Leviticus and then proceeded to *burn the Bible* he was reading from.

In the "News Watch" column of *TV Guide* for the first week in September Kevin Phillips observed: ". . . press reports indicate that June's Gay Pride Day events in Boston included some transvestite flamenco dancers performing in a local cemetery. Do gays *really* want full minority-cum-subculture attention on television news—or wouldn't it be better to minimize coverage across the board?"

We know that the world ridicules us when we speak of receiving guidance from God. But we who understand the total ramifications of what this nation is facing must continue to seek that guidance. We do not hold it against the scoffers who attempt to make us sound holier-than-thou and super-pious. The Bible says of them:

> But the man who isn't a Christian can't understand and can't accept these thoughts from God, which the Holy Spirit teaches us. They sound foolish to him, because only those who have the Holy Spirit within them can understand what the Holy Spirit means. Others just can't take it in.

> But the spiritual man has insight into everything, and that bothers and baffles the man of the world, who can't understand him at all. How could he?

> For certainly he has never been one to know the Lord's thoughts, or to discuss them with him, or to move the hands of God by prayer. But, strange as it seems, we Christians actually do have within us a portion of the very thoughts and mind of Christ.
> 1 Corinthians 2:14–16 LB

Time magazine (August 29, 1977) reported that in July ". . . some 100 gay activists converged on a Manhattan bar where an ax was suspended from the wall with a wooden plaque beneath it labeled FAIRY SWATTER." The gays insisted on its destruction. The home of Adam Walinsky who had written an article which questioned a special law protective of homosexuals was attacked by about fifty gays. ". . . they cut the telephone lines to the house, pelted it with eggs, set off firecrackers, and chanted through bullhorns: 'Walinsky, you liar/We'll set your house on fire.' . . . Asks Walinsky: 'Why do people who claim to want human rights go around like a bunch of Storm Troopers trying to intimidate others from expressing their views?' "

There is so much I could share with you, so much I have learned these past difficult months. God has been *so* faithful. As a silent majority we are ineffectual, but if we continue to pool our efforts and resources as Christians and as morally concerned Americans to proclaim what we know and believe to be right, we can reverse the trend that militant homosexuals and others are working to force upon us. Join us in accepting the challenge and acting together to protect America's children.

He [Jesus] carries out and fulfills all of God's promises, no matter how many of them there are; and we have told everyone how faithful he is, giving glory to his name.

It is this God who has made you and me into faithful Christians and commissioned us . . . to preach the Good News.

He has put his brand upon us—his mark of ownership—and given us his Holy Spirit in our hearts as guarantee that we belong to him . . . .

I call upon this God to witness against me if I am not telling the absolute truth . . . .

2 Corinthians 1:20–23 LB

Appendix of Media Coverage

I. "Joining the Bryant Brigade," Dr. Max Rafferty, Los Angeles *Times*

II. *The Truth Is God's Word . . . . The Holy Bible Says,* Bulletin distributed at the God and Decency Rally

III. "The Civil Rights of Parents: To Save Their Children From Homosexual Influence," advertisement in Miami newspapers sponsored by Save Our Children, Inc.

IV. "Anita Bryant: Convenient Kicking Object for Boobs and Hysterics," Bob Roberts, KIXI, Seattle, Washington

I

Joining the Bryant Brigade

Now that the smoke has cleared from last month's big shoot-out in the Dade County corral, let's take a closer look at one aspect of Anita Bryant.

The lady is, incidentally, a phenomenon—that rarest of rare birds these days: a female entertainer willing to stand up to the vilest and most scurrilous kind of public abuse for the sake of morality, simple decency and Holy Scripture. But it's the "one aspect" I want to zero in on.

Anita doesn't want her children taught in tax-supported public schools by sex perverts.

Neither do I. Do you?

Here's why I'm lining up in the Bryant Brigade. Not because I want any American denied his or her constitutional rights. Not because I want particularly to be beastly to the bisexual or nasty to the nance. No, it's because children—especially young children—reason this way, and you'd better believe it:

"Mom and Dad tell me to mind the teacher, to listen carefully to what she tells me. So what she does and what she is must be okay, fine and dandy."

But what the homosexual teacher does and is are most emphatically not okay, fine or dandy at all. Such people, whether willingly or unwillingly, are abnormal by the very definition of the word.

The ancient Jews who wrote the Torah used an interesting term to identify the act of sodomy: "confusion."

That's what it is, you know. Confusion of the sex roles. Confusion of the biological purpose behind the sex act. Confusion of masculinity with femininity. Confusion thrice confounded.

My point: American classrooms are currently perplexed, bewildered, befogged, jumbled and muddled enough, Lord knows, without turning them over to super-confused homosexuals who will willy-nilly escalate existing obfuscation into total chaos.

For eight eventful years, I chaired the statewide credentials commission of the most populous state in the land. Our job in large part was to decide each month whether certain teachers were mentally or morally fit to be allowed to teach in California public schools.

And from the beginning we took for granted the premise that a homosexual in a school job was as out of the question as a heroin addict working in a drugstore.

Why? As long as the deviate doesn't flaunt his deviation at school or on school time, isn't he as entitled to be a teacher as say—a paraplegic or an epileptic?

Nope. Neither the paraplegic nor the epileptic is violating moral and religious laws which go back to the very childhood of the human race. They are physically afflicted, not morally alienated.

The homosexual, on the other hand, is apart—separate—spiritually isolated from the deepest instincts of homosapiens. It may not be his fault. It may be regrettable—sad—even tragic. But it's true.

And school children catch on inevitably and quickly. Little pitchers have big ears, as our forebears were fond of saying, and it's still true. Their reasoning is stark in its simplicity and as certain as sunrise: "If it's okay to hire a pervert to teach in a public institution and if it's okay to pay a pervert with tax money and if it's okay to put a pervert in charge of the educational destinies of school children, then it must be okay to be a pervert."

This, fellow Americans, we simply cannot have. We cannot have it because the actual survival of our country in the years ahead depends upon a generation which will be straight, not distorted—sensible, not absurd.

Where do I sign up for the duration, General Bryant?

DR. MAX RAFFERTY

II

The Truth Is God's Word . . . .
The Holy Bible Says

1. HOMOSEXUALITY AND LESBIAN ACTS ARE:
   A. Abominations (Leviticus 18:1–30)
2. GOD GAVE THEM UP:
   A. Without excuse (Romans 1:20–28)
   B. Change the glory of the uncorruptible God
   C. Vile affection
   D. Unnatural
   E. Reprobate mind (Proverbs 11:3)
   F. Perversion (Proverbs 12:8)
3. CRY ALOUD, SPARE NOT, LIFT UP THY VOICE LIKE A TRUMPET & SHOW MY PEOPLE THEIR TRANSGRESSION: (Isaiah 58:1)
   A. SHEPHERDS: Does each member know your position on this, and if not, why not?
   B. PASTORS: Do you feel the urgency of the hour?
   C. PRIEST: Is the Spirit stirring you to do something?
   D. EVANGELIST: Don't be silent; speak out.
   E. RABBI: Be another Isaiah.
   F. TEACHER: Let not the blind lead the blind.
   G. ELECTED OFFICIALS: Local, County, State and Federal—now is your time to let the people know where you stand. Do stand and be counted for righteousness of God and for your Country.
   H. LAYMEN: Be thy brother's keeper.
   I. REDEEMED ONES: Let the redeemed of the Lord say so.
   J. BELIEVERS: Be steadfast, unmovable, always abounding in the work of the Lord.
   K. GOOD MORAL PERSONS: Work to protect your morals.
   L. GOOD CITIZEN: Vote and encourage others to vote.

M. FATHER & MOTHER: Raise up your child in the nurture and admonition of the Lord.

4. WILL GOD SPARE MIAMI & DADE COUNTY IF HE SPARED NOT THE PEOPLE IN THE CITIES OF SODOM & GOMOR-RAH? (Genesis 18:1–33)
   A. Abominable (Revelation 21:8)
   B. Effeminate (I Corinthians 6:9–10)
   C. Ashamed (Jeremiah 8:12)
   D. Reproof (Proverbs 1:7)

5. IS THERE ANY HOPE FOR HOMOSEXUALS? (I Corinthians 6:9–11)
   A. Repentance
   B. The fear of the Lord (Proverbs 1:23–32)
   C. Pray for their salvation during these days.

6. The burden has been put on us to sound the alarm, cry aloud to preserve our heritage which our forefathers handed down to us as they honored God and put laws on the books of our State that stand with the word of God, those which prohibit this "Homosexual Ordinance" that our County Commissioners voted into law.

7. If we are truly leaders who stand for the honorable, clean, wholesome way of life for God and Country, let us not fail to pray, talk, proclaim, admonish, call, pass out literature, speak on radio or TV, write newspaper articles, contact elected officials, etc. We must do all we can to stir up the people as to the importance of getting out to vote on June 7, to defeat this ordinance. Should we fail, we fear God's judgement as it was in the cities of Sodom and Gomorrah. Let us honor God and pray that others will see our faith and our fear of His judgement by the way we work to defeat this ordinance, so God's blessing will be upon Miami and all of Dade County.

8. The golden opportunity is ours, so let us work every hour and every day possible until the victory is our Lord's. God bless you as we endeavor to occupy until our Lord Jesus comes again.

Vote FOR Repeal !!!

III

The Civil Rights of Parents: To Save Their Children From Homosexual Influence

Homosexuality is nothing new. Cultures throughout history, moreover, have dealt with homosexuals almost universally with disdain, abhorrence, disgust—even death.

While times certainly have changed, and American society largely has developed an attitude of tolerance, that tolerance toward homosexuality is based on the understanding that homosexuals will keep their deviate activity to themselves, will not flaunt their lifestyles, will not be allowed to preach their sexual standards to, or otherwise influence, impressionable young people.

That attitude of tolerance, most unfortunately, recently was destroyed in this community by the Metropolitan Dade County Commission, which voted, in effect, to legitimize homosexuals' presence in our society—by forcing our private and religious schools to accept them as teachers, by forcing property owners and employers to open their doors to homosexuals no matter how blatant their perverted lives may be.

CIVIL WRONGS VS. CIVIL RIGHTS

Homosexual acts are illegal under Florida law and the laws of most states. The Metro Commission, nevertheless, chose to ignore the spirit of our laws and caved in to a small, vocal group of "gays." (Interestingly, Webster's third definition of "gay" is "licentious,"

145

which further is defined as "lacking legal or moral restraints; disregarding sexual restraints; marked by disregard of rules.")

Despite the obvious fact that homosexual acts *are* illegal—and, in the eyes of most people, immoral—some *non*-homosexual supporters of the homosexuals' point of view contend that the issue is one of "civil rights."

Metro's blundering "gay" ordinance is no more a civil rights issue than is the arrest of a drunk for disturbing the peace. (Former U.S. Senator Sam Ervin of North Carolina—considered by many to be one of the finest constitutional lawyers in the nation—wrote after the Metro passage, "I am certainly surprised that any public official in America would vote for such an ordinance.")

In fact the leaders of the homosexuals in testifying before the Metro Commission, repeatedly bragged that they "already are here" . . . in jobs, in schools, in every conceivable niche. They further stated that they had not suffered discrimination.

Why no discrimination? Because, until *now,* they kept their sexual deviation private, and, thus, no one except their own kind knew or cared about their "affectional preference."

INVITATION TO RECRUIT OUR CHILDREN

That has all been changed by Metro. Unless repealed, the ordinance will allow homosexuals, as one leader has promised, to provide "role models" for the impressionable—that is, the right to tell all society, especially our youth, that homosexuality isn't wrong, just "different" . . . and, of course, "gay."

This recruitment of our children is absolutely necessary for the survival and growth of homosexuality—for since homosexuals cannot reproduce, they *must* recruit, *must* freshen their ranks. And who qualifies as a likely recruit: a 35-year-old father or mother of two . . . or a teenage boy or girl who is surging with sexual awareness? (The Los Angeles Police Department recently reported that 25,000 boys 17 years old or younger in that city alone have been recruited into a homosexual ring to provide sex for adult male customers. One boy, just 12 years old, was described as a $1,000-a-day prostitute.)

WHAT CAN BE DONE . . . AND HAS BEEN DONE

On the heels of the passage of the Metro homosexual recruitment ordinance, a diverse group of citizens joined forces to organize Save Our Children, Inc., a nonprofit corporation under Florida law. Organizers included whites, blacks, Spanish-speaking, Protestants, Catholics, Jews, Greek Orthodox, non-religious, Democrats, Republicans, political independents, liberals and conservatives.

The breadth and depth of Save Our Children, Inc., became apparent several days ago when the organization presented more than 60,000 citizens' names on petitions to the Metro Commission—believed to be the most signatures ever collected by petition in Metro history in such a short time (three weeks), and 50,000 signatures more than were needed to put the ordinance on the ballot for repeal. The Commission subsequently put the issue of repeal on the ballot for a special countywide election to be conducted Tuesday, June 7.

What is needed now is for you to speak out.

Save Our Children, Inc., urges you and your family and friends to write Dade County newspaper editors and other members of local news media (radio and TV) with your opinion on the subject of the homosexual recruitment ordinance. Likewise, you are urged to contact your friends and family to urge them to vote for repeal of the ordinance June 7.

ONLY THE BEGINNING

It is imperative that the Metro ordinance be repealed June 7. The entire nation . . . The Normal Majority . . . will be watching the results of this campaign and the election.

Yet, even if the ordinance is repealed, the battle of parents to protect their children from homosexuality has not ended, for, at this moment, in the Congress of the United States, 25 misguided congressmen are pushing a bill (H.R. 2998) which would impose *on the entire nation* the same dangers found in Metro's law.

The bill in Congress actually goes even further than Metro's new ordinance, for under the provisions of H.R. 2998, *all public schools would be compelled to hire homosexuals as teachers,* and the military likewise could not reject homosexual applicants.

Save Our Children urges you also to write your congressman—Dante Fascell (15th District), Claude Pepper (14th) or Bill Lehman (13th)—at the U.S. House of Representatives, Washington, D.C., to protest the passage of H.R. 2998.

THE PRICE OF SAVING OUR CHILDREN

This message, prepared for the people of Dade County, is expensive to publish in our daily Miami newspapers—but no cost is too great to save our children, and we are grateful to the many hundreds of concerned parents who have contributed to this cause. (Note: Our income and expenses will be fully reported to the Office of the Secretary of State in Tallahassee, as required by law.)

Your children are precious assets to you and our nation. Please help us protect them, with your prayers, your active participation . . . and your financial contribution today.

ANITA BRYANT, President
Save Our Children, Inc.

BOB BRAKE, Secretary,
Save Our Children, Inc.

IV

Anita Bryant:
Convenient Kicking Object for
Boobs and Hysterics

Echoes of the Dade County, Florida, war rumble on, and Anita Bryant, the Orange Juice girl who became chief protagonist on the side of the victors, emerges as a composite Lucrezia Borgia and Madame Defarge: Militant piety in a Jacobin cap.

Miss Bryant is accused of fomenting mass hysteria; of bringing shame upon the nation; of engineering, unassisted, a massive defeat of democracy, and of single-handedly thrusting the country back into the dark ages.

Mercy me! One small lady did that?

One frenzied letter to our leading herald here in Seattle manages somehow to link Miss Bryant with the anti-Chinese "hysteria" that allegedly overtook the whole country at the turn of the century, the Japanese "exclusion act" of the 1920s (it wasn't exclusion; it was an entry quota), the Japanese resettlement act of World War II, and something the writer calls the "expatriation" of Filipinos. Maybe she means repatriation, which is decidedly different.

"Will this country never free itself of this mass hysteria?" the writer asks. "Must every generation shield its children from those few individuals who can tolerate nothing that does not incorporate their own life style . . . ?"

Talk about hysteria! Now, honestly, does any reasonable person really suppose Anita Bryant managed all that? Isn't it just possible that the homosexual community is itself responsible in large measure for this controversy? After all, no one paid them much attention, on the job or off, until they started jabbering publicly about their sex lives, like the cretins in television and the movies who suppose their bedroom activities are somehow of interest to, or the business of, everyone else.

And just what did Anita Bryant do anyway, apart from persuasively speaking her piece from her point of view? She wasn't the issue, nor were her fundamentalist beliefs the issue.

The issue was an ill-considered ordinance that proposed to tell employers whom they must hire, not on the basis of aptitude and qualification for the job, but on the basis of sexual preference, habit or aberration. Had the ordinance not been defeated, how long does one suppose it would have taken the bureaucrats to establish quotas for such hiring? And who would be next in line demanding their rights? the sado-masochists and the cult of bestiality?

If this country would try to get its collective mind out of its groin for five minutes it might recognize that the issue in this melancholy wrangle wasn't Anita Bryant or the rights of homosexuals. It was another blatant attempt by government to impose improper rules and restrictions upon free men and women.

The ordinance was bad law; and it was repealed because it was bad law.

Anita Bryant is only a convenient kicking object for the hysterical.

> BOB ROBERTS
> KIXI
> Seattle, Washington
> July 12, 1977

Acknowledgments

I know the reader can appreciate the difficulty I encounter as I attempt to thank the vast number of people who worked with us in the Save Our Children Dade County campaign. But I must acknowledge these people and others who were supportive in various ways. There will be those who are inadvertently omitted; I ask your understanding and forgiveness—it is not intentional.

Save Our Children Officers: Secretary Robert M. Brake, councilman of the City of Coral Gables; Treasurer Bob Green. Vice Presidents: Rabbi Phineas Weberman, secretary of the Rabbinical Council of Greater Miami; Rev. Charles Couey, pastor of South Dade Baptist Church in Homestead; Rev. F. William Chapman, my own beloved pastor at Northwest Baptist Church; Chet Fields, then a Miami Springs councilman—recently elected mayor of Miami Springs; Alvin Dark, former manager of the Oakland A's and now manager of the San Diego Padres; Joseph Fitzgerald, attorney and official representative for the late Archbishop Coleman Carroll; Rev. Joe Coats, Baptist minister, and his official representative Rev. Joseph Betsy; Dr. Jose Borrell, president of the YMCA International; Mrs. Magaly Llaguno, founder of the Spanish Right to Life movement and director of the Catholic League for Civil and Religious Rights; Rabbi Tozi Schur and Carlos Arboleya.

Directors: Judi Wilson, president of Concerned Christian Mothers; Evelyn Galvin and her husband Bill, founder of Cedars of Lebanon Diagnostic Clinic; Ginny Harlan, member of the Catholic Women's Club; Monty Weinstein, former member of the State Community Relations Commission; Ernie Fanotto, president of Dade County Voters and Taxpayers League; Stanley (president of The Mail Room)

151

and Joy Cole; Bob Skidell, president of Miami Beach Lodge of B'nai B'rith; Mike Thompson, of Long Advertising; and Bob Daly, retired newspaperman.

Special thanks to Magaly Llaguno without whose help we could never have obtained the overwhelming support we received from the Latin community.

Save Our Children Office Workers and Volunteers: Tim Baer, Susan Nay, Cathy Ellis (who wrote the song "Lord, Save Our Children"); Julie Packer, Debbie Sullivan (Bob's faithful and uncomplaining secretary); Jackie Lee (who literally closed the Fishers of Men office to work full time for SOC); Della Fugate, Gwen Snyder, Rudy Wilson, Edsel and Toni Ganey, Lynnell Hitchcock, Peggy Chapman, Tom and Marie Palmer (Archdiocese of Catholic Women); Helen (past president of the Dade County Federation of Women's Clubs) and Wyatt Crane, Shirley and Ken Harris, Mr. and Mrs. Fred Herne, Charlie and Fredda Walker (who went beyond the call of duty in caring for our family); our dear friend Jody Dunton (who worked in the SOC office on her days off and helped with our family); Pedro (our handyman) and his wife Susie Vasquez; Gladys Silva, Mr. and Mrs. Al Masso, Edwin Frey, Mrs. Robert Acher, Mrs. Joseph Donahue (representing the Catholic Women's Club); Mrs. Betty LueBien (president of Women for Responsible Legislation—Dade County Chapter); Bill Runde (of Commercial Printers); James and Diane Davison, Debbie Robinson; special thanks to Juan and Norma Parron, Theo Sherman, Norma and Jack Carnes, Dot Jones, Marie Jacobson, Bill Mitchell, Monsignor Joseph Fogarty, Arlene Grimes (Here's Life); a special thank you to John Sorenson, Joy Voll, Kathy Miller, Pat and Don Atkinson, Chuck and Peggy Walker, Jerry and Elaine Kranz, Pat and Buddy Phillips, Jean Melonis, Tom and Marge Ruggerio, Penny and Ed Adams, Nancy Girard, Jim Snyder, Jim Whitaker, Roy Fraysier, Warren Howell, Ernestine Mauk, Virgil Pool, Mary White, Diane Stine, Ilene Green, Ruth May, Walter and Faith Nix, Jeff and Charles Marceline, John Collins, Jim Collier, Mildred Cox, Vic DiFrisco, Bud and Sharon Hill (Northwest Baptist friends); the Northwest Baptist Church family, Richard and Marty Campbell, Bill Evans, Art Melonis, Bob Palmer, Harold Poirier (more Northwest friends); Bob and Phyllis Falco, Mrs. Lillian Gold-green (with the Synagogue of Women in Dade County); Rev. Martine Anorga (pastor of the First Spanish Presbyterian Church and School); Dr. Maria Crespi, Felix Cruz, Emilia Gutierrez, Helen Leapold, Jerry Bauhman, "Grandma" Berry, Tom Sobeck, Gracy Read, Bev Reagon, Katie Gaither, Eleanor Clowney, Earl and Arlene Duame, Barbara Parns, Alice Knight, Ellis and Eileen Ruben, Barbara Walker, and all who were in our speakers' bureau; Mary Bishop, Jean McVey, Britt Snowden, Kay Cooper, Helen and Earl Culbreth, Betty Hart, Doris Stafford, Doris Whitmore, Beth Paul, Gertrude Conners, Doris Martucci, Al Pacatti, Joann and Ken Jewett, Janet Singleton, Ruth Whitson, Marion and Jack Connors, John and Ollie Thomas, Lily Stone, Jack Owen Ward, John Kerns, Tom and Jeanne Scarborough, Adon Taft, Mr. and Mrs. Ray Lovell, Bill and Barbara O'Neil, Allen Morris, Bob LaPlant, Tom Lacey, Robert Cannady, Roger Redford, Paul Duame, John and Dorothy Baker, Oswald McIntyre, Anne Verrochi, Charlie Morgan, Jr., Ray Morgan, Mr. and Mrs. Charles Morgan, Sr., Charlotte and Al Allen, Al Chubb, Nancy Vanderhider, Huntsinger and Jeffer.

Supportive Media: Mr. and Mrs. James Rice, Bernice and Mr. and Mrs. Alan Courtney (WINZ Radio); Channel 4 (WTVJ) and Ralph Renick; Ed Hall of the *Good News* paper and *The Catholic Voice;* Adil Even of Channel 51 ("Tele-Hogar"); Jim Treloar of Detroit *News;* Dr. Horacro Aquirre, editor *Diario Las Americas;* Radio Station WMCU, Kenneth Gangel, president of Miami Christian College; Ted Place and Larry Zagray of WMCU; Rev. John Huffman, Sr., who helped greatly on "Commission Concern," his program on WIOD radio; Lester Summeral of TV Channel 45; Zennin Hansen, Brian Holloway, John Phelan, M.D., Shirley Spellerburg of WKAT; *Christian Life* magazine, *Baptist Messenger and Journal, Presbyterian Layman,* Youth Sunday School Literature; John Huddy and Jack Roberts with the Miami *Herald;* The *Sun Reporter* of Miami Beach; The Miami *News;* John McMullan, executive editor Miami *Herald.* Thanks to "The 700 Club" and Pat Robertson; "The PTL Club" and Jim Bakker; Phyllis Schlafly, Gail Smith (who did a beautiful job as my pianist); Pat Macauly, Jack Connors, Dr. Jerry Falwell and "The Old Time Gospel Hour"; Bill Faulkner, Dr. Jack Wyrtzen, his secretaries and staff, all the people who helped with the great "God and Decency Rally."

All clergy and members of the churches and synagogues in Dade County and all over the nation who stood up with us during the election; Jim Benton of the Caribbean Evangelistic Baptist Association, Eduardo Hernandez of the Northside Spanish Baptist Church, Eugene Gonzales of Northwest Baptist Church, W. A. Criswell of the First Baptist Church of Dallas, Dr. and Mrs. Jim Kennedy and the members of Coral Ridge Presbyterian Church, Rev. John Pistone of the Miami Baptist Church Association, Rev. Thedford Johnson of St. John's Baptist Church, Rev. Bob Gray of Trinity Baptist Church in Jacksonville, Bishop James Duncann, Rev. E. Castaneda, Rev. Joseph Floreck, Dr. Robert McGee, Rabbis Dov Bidnik, Sheldon Ever, Abraham Groner, Alexander Kors, Shalom B. Libsker, Zev Leff, Dow Rosenwaig, Elizer Rokack, Milton Simon, Mordecai Shapiro, Tibor H. Svern, Yockanon Zweig, Irving Lehrman, Alexander Gross.

Political and Civic Group Support: Florida Governor Reubin Askew, Dade County Mayor Steve Clark, Dade County Commissioners Clara Oesterle and Neal Adams, Mayor E. Clay Shaw, Jr., of Fort Lauderdale, John Stembridge, Mr. and Mrs. Bruce Smathers (Florida Secretary of State); Mr. and Mrs. Bill Gunter, New Orleans District Attorney Harry Connick, Civic Action Committee of Miami Beach, Fraternal Order of Police and Associates, Mayor Moon Landrieu of New Orleans, Citizens for Constructive Education, Lewis Sabines (president of the Latin Chamber of Commerce); the Kiwanis Clubs and civic organizations across Florida and the nation who sent us supporting resolutions; all the police and security personnel throughout the nation responsible for our well-being.

U.S. Senators Jesse Helms and Sam Ervin; State Senators Alan Trask, William G. Zinkill, Sr., Curtis Peterson (Florida); Mary Helm (Oklahoma); Walter Mengden (Texas); Marion (Mike) Menning (Minnesota); John Briggs (California); State Representatives Clay Smothers (Texas); George Hansen (Idaho); Elaine Bloom and Sherman Winn (Florida); Lane A. Carson (Louisiana); Richard Kelley (Illinois); Edward Gearty and George Vaughn and those senators who voted against the ERA: Lew Brantley (D); Dempsey Barron (D); W. D. Childers (D); Tom Gallen (D); Bill Gorman (R); Warren S. Henderson (R); Vernon Holloway (D); Philip D. Lewis (D); David H. McClain (R); Kenneth A. Plante (R); Ralph R. Poston (D); Richard R. Renick (D); Henry B. Fayler (R); James A. Scott (R); Pat Thomas (D); Tom Tobiassen (R); John T. Ware (R); George Williamson (R); William G. Zinkil, Sr. (D).

Prayer and Letter Supporters: Rev. and Mrs. Oral Roberts, Dr. and Mrs. Billy Graham, Pat Boone, Dale Evans and Roy Rogers, Dr. Bill Bright (Campus Crusade International); Del Fehsenfeld, Tom Ellis, John Carbaugh, Mr. and Mrs. Dean Jones, Mr. and Mrs. Len Le Sourd (Catherine Marshall); The Life Action Team, the Hume Lake Christian Camps, comedian Jerry Clower, Gloria (Roe) and Ron Robertson, Youth for Christ, National Gospel Ministries (Tustin, CA); Youth With a Mission School of Evangelism (Solvang, CA); The National Association of Pro-America, Word of Life Fellowship, Inc., secretaries and directors; Ann and Frank Wanicka, sheriff of Lee County and his Cops for Christ, Cecil Todd, Revival Fires, Evangelist J. Harold Smith, Chuck Colson, Massachusetts Women for Constitutional Government, Citizens for Decency Through Law, Inc., National Right to Life Committee, the Women's Interdenominational Prayer Group of Madison, Indiana, Christian Civic Foundation, Inc., Art DeMoss of National Liberty Corp., Christian Purities Fellowship, National Gospel Ministries, and many more we can't begin to name.

Churches across the nation responded. In addition to the mainline denominations, the Church of Latter-Day Saints (Salt Lake City), the Orthodox Church, the Friends Church.

Seattle Businessmen, the People of Anchorage, Alaska, the Full Gospel Businessmen's groups nationwide, many Christian schools across the land, city-government representatives, all of the many Florida churches who wrote, called and sent telegrams, all of the Sunday-school classes, church and civic groups who signed their names to letters, especially my class of eleven-year-olds; substitute teacher Christine Porter and the junior 6A department, the student bodies, faculty and staff of colleges, universities and seminaries throughout the country; a special thanks to the "Idaho men of the cloth"—the clergy.

God's blessing and gratitude to all the gals who were part of my home prayer group, and to our local and worldwide prayer-chain partners. Also to Mr. and Mrs. Mark Rust, Mr. and Mrs. Claughton Anthony Abraham, John Beatty, Alex P. Courtelis, Alberto Alejandre, Armer E. White and Gertrude Porter. Heartfelt thanks to the Florida Citrus Commission and Florida Citrus Growers, and First Federal of Miami who believed in our rights as private citizens.

To all those others who served with us during the campaign in Miami, many of whom we disagree with on many issues, political and otherwise, but, who are united with us in the preservation of the American family unit and the attacks on this unit by certain militant segments of our society.